A RINGING CALL
TO MISSION

A RINGING CALL
TO MISSION *Alan Walker*

ABINGDON PRESS
New York Nashville

A RINGING CALL TO MISSION

Copyright © 1966 by Abingdon Press

Library of Congress Catalog Card Number: 66-10852

SET UP, PRINTED, AND BOUND BY THE
PARTHENON PRESS, AT NASHVILLE,
TENNESSEE, UNITED STATES OF AMERICA

TO MY WIFE, WINIFRED
in love and gratitude

CONTENTS

CONTENTS

The Inescapable Call to Mission

A ringing call to mission is sounding throughout the Christian world. It comes directly from the compassionate mind and heart of God. It rises in response to the individual needs of men and women confused and lost in a secular society. It offers deliverance amid nuclear danger and despair. It is the essence of the Christian gospel. To all who would obey the living God comes an inescapable call to mission.

The supreme purpose of the Christian church is always that of reaching men and women with the good news of Jesus Christ. In this kind of age, mission takes on a new urgency. Unless there is a multiplication of Christians, other ministries of the church will remain unfulfilled. Without people who desire Christian understanding, Christian educational programs cannot function. Unless a passion for mission throbs through the reunion movement, church union appears to be Christians trying to huddle together in trouble, seeking amalgamations through ne-cessity and defeatism. Social service, without an underly-ing sense of mission, looks like the church turning to welfare activities, because the offering of a full gospel has become too difficult. Mission—first, last, and always—is the basic, thrilling purpose of everything Christian.

What has gone wrong with many of us as Christians? Has our faith in the supremacy of Christ faltered? Have we lost our nerve? Are we so conditioned by indifference or opposition that we no longer witness with confidence?

Pessimism, timidity, and defeatism are just plain faith-lessness. Yet how far the mood has seeped. It is heard in England and Europe in the much-used, chilling phrase "post-Christian society." It appears in the catacomb men-tality which would retreat into the tiny concept of the "house church." It lies beneath the intellectual uncer-tainty of Christians who almost give the impression that the gospel is scarcely credible in an age of science.

With a loss of confidence, gaiety and gladness have de-parted. Among many Christians the joy of salvation has disappeared. Christian worship has so often become drab and dull. The singing is dreary, the pace of worship tired and uninspired, the prayers stale and couched in a lan-guage of unreality. The prophetic voice of the church is muted, as the gospel is adjusted to the surrounding cul-ture. Only in low and mumbled voice is the mighty decla-ration heard—"Christ is risen."

Again, I say, what has gone wrong with us as Chris-tians? In God's name why cannot we proclaim with boldness the faith we hold? If anyone emerges from the

10

testing of these years with his reputation unruined it is Jesus Christ.

No apologies, please, for the Christian gospel. Tell it, tell it on the mountains, tell it in the plains, tell it in the cities. Tell it, wherever people are found. Tell to the whole wide world that Jesus Christ is Savior and Lord.

Why has mission become imperative? What are the compelling reasons which drive the Christian out today with particular urgency in evangelism? These are real questions, and must be answered.

The Christian facts of life support the call for mission. Masses of people within Christendom, and beyond, live and die without a knowledge of Christ. Is not this reason enough?

The Christian map of the world today shows strange and contrasting features. In some areas it is dark and depressing. In others it is filled with light.

Christendom, as a geographic entity, has almost disappeared. Once Christendom stretched from the Russian snows to the warm waters of the Mediterranean and outward into the new world of America and Australia. Now, especially in Europe, disintegration is far developed.

Russia is officially atheistic, although it must never be forgotten that there are fifty million people within Russia who remain linked with the Christian church. In Sweden only three per cent of the people attend church. The Archbishop of Milan has said that France must be regarded as a missionary field all over again.

In England the picture is depressing. Only two per cent of the people go to church in London on a given Sunday, seven per cent in England as a whole, nine per cent if

Scotland is included. It is a startling thought that today probably more people go to church in Moscow than London. Fifty years ago the Free Church membership in England was 2,000,000. Today it is 1,500,000, although the population over the period has increased by 12,000,000.

No one can look at the great traditional centers of Christian strength from which the faith has moved out to the rest of the world without disappointment and concern. With the industrial masses alienated from the church and the intellectual classes skeptical of religious faith in an age of scientific humanism, the proclamation of the Christian gospel is difficult. Two world wars and the circumstances of a mass society have eroded the life of faith.

There is another side to the picture. Look the other way and the land is bright. At the very time when an old Christendom was dying, a new one was being born. For the last two hundred years God has been fashioning a new community of faith. It cannot be defined in geographic terms, yet it encircles the globe, as for the first time the Christian faith has taken root among little communities of people in every land. So Nathaniel Micklem can write in *The Creed of a Christian:* "Never since the first age has the Cross of Christ won such triumphs as in these years, so much that if Christianity were to die out in Europe and America, it lives in Asia, is established in Africa and the islands of the southern seas."

What is happening on the American continent cannot be ignored. If the place of the church in society has been shrinking in England and Europe, it has been expanding in the United States. In 1964 sixty-four per cent of the people were members of one or another of the churches, the highest percentage level ever reached. Minimizing the significance of the "religious boom" in America to the utmost, there are positive facts of strength to be faced.

The spread of a personal, vital religious life in South America is another of the Christian world facts to be placed on the credit side of the ledger. The growth of the Pentecostal movement there is one of the strange events of the Christian world scene.

From the emergence of a new Christendom has come the ecumenical movement. Its significance has not been better expressed than by William Temple in his Enthronement Sermon at Canterbury in 1942: "As though in preparation for such a time as this, God has been building up a Christian fellowship which now extends into almost every nation. . . . Almost incidentally the great world-fellowship has arisen; it is the great new fact of our era."

From the world population explosion rises the call to mission. If people matter to God, if a knowledge of Christ is as important as Christians claim, the church is facing its greatest challenge since the first century.

Look at the bare facts. It took from the birth of Christ until about the year 1620 for the population of the world to double from 250 million to 500 million people. Since 1620, and especially with the coming of the Industrial Revolution, the population has climbed with astonishing speed. Now it has reached 3,000 million people and, if present trends continue, only thirty years will be required for the figure of 6,000 million to be reached.

Within this world trend Christianity is not numerically

holding its own. In 1900 Christians made up 32.2 per cent of the world's population. Although their number had increased from 500 million to 850 million by 1960, the percentage of Christians in the world had fallen to 30.3 per cent. The fallacy of even this figure can be seen from the fact that among that 850 million Christians virtually the whole population of England, America, and Australia were counted.

Every generation must be won to Christ. In one sense the world always stands only one generation away from a reversion to paganism. How then can the absurd comment ever be heard that the missionary era is finished? With two thirds of the human family knowing nothing of the Christian story, with that number increasing daily, has the missionary era really begun? The world population explosion calls irresistably to mission.

From the very heart of Christian faith rises the call, no, the demand, to go on mission. There lie the urgency, the motive, the purpose, the power for mission.

The motive, the urgency for mission, must today be reexpressed. After all, the older motive for evangelism has largely died. Whence came that former urgency? From belief in hell.

The picture was simple. Men and women, unless reconciled to God in Christ by the moment of death, fell into the tortures of hell, from which there was no escape. So with passion and urgency our forefathers sought to "pluck the brand from the burning."

This belief has gone. Even where ideas of an everlasting hell linger, the eternal consequences of the rejection of Christ are proclaimed with muted voice. The idea of God which most Christians hold today has made belief in an endless hell of torment impossible. How can God out-Himmler Himmler and create an eternal concentration camp of torture from which there can be no reprieve? While sin still brings its consequences here and in an afterlife, to load on to the moment of death so great a significance is without moral and spiritual justification. Likewise the picture of an everlasting hell simply does not square with the total picture of God revealed in his Son Jesus Christ.

What substitute motive for urgency can be found? It lies in the fact that it is God's will that his Son should be known on earth. If we believe that obedience to God is central to faith, is not this motive enough?

Urgency and compassion rise from realizing what it means to live without Christ. Religion used to be related to the moment of dying; now it must be related to the moment of living. Death has receded. While still suddenly —on the roads, in the air—we can in the midst of life be in the midst of death, yet the lengthening of life's expectancy has changed the thinking of us all. When twenty-seven or twenty-eight was the average life expectancy, death was a consciously realized fact. Such is not the case today, when most of us expect to live to a ripe old age of seventy or eighty years.

To go on living apart from an acceptance of the love of God is the real tragedy. Surely our hearts ache for our splendid youth when we think of them, not dying, but living apart from knowing life to the full in Christ. To continue a day, a month, a year, a decade without Christ is cause enough for sorrow. We surely want to shout the words of Shakespeare in *Othello* concerning unnecessary tragedy: "Oh, the pity of it, the pity of it."

Urgency rises when we remember we may not have endless time to proclaim the Christian gospel. Jesus once said: "We must work the works of him who sent me, while it is day; night comes when no one can work" (John 9:4). I have always interpreted these words in a very personal way. I shall presently become frail and old and cannot go out to preach the good news.

There is another meaning. The night can come when the Christian shall not be permitted to preach the gospel. Such a time has come in China. No longer can the missionary enter China. The indigenous church lives on. Yet had the Christian world known that the barriers would arise, how much more urgent would have been the witness when the way was open.

Already restrictions are rising in other lands. In Malaya it is an offense to change religion. In Ceylon no increase in missionaries is permitted. D. T. Niles prophesies that in fifteen years the doors could close in India.

Nor should we say freedom to preach will remain in so-called Christian lands. Anywhere, everywhere the moment could come when the proclamation of a total gospel, at once personal and social, could face restrictions. Preach urgently while there is time. This is the word which comes to us. The night could come when the church will not be permitted to preach.

In a nuclear age another threat hangs above humanity. The night of nuclear war, black, impenetrable, could descend on history. Neither the proclaimer nor the hearer of the gospel could be here. There is not endless time to declare: "God so loved the world that he gave his only Son, that whoever believes in him should not perish but have eternal life" (John 3:16).

The Spirit of God does not send us out into the world to witness; rather from that world he calls us to join him. D. T. Niles put it this way when he spoke at the New Delhi Assembly of the World Council of Churches: "God is previous to him who witnesses in the life of the person whom he is seeking to win for the gospel, and also previous in whatever area of life he is seeking to make the gospel effective."

In Petru Dumitriu's novel *Incognito,* the central character is a Rumanian named Sebastian Ionesco. His search for the meaning of life leads him in protest to turn from the sensuality and triviality of Rumanian society. He enlists in the army to fight against Soviet Russia in the Second World War. Captured by the Russians, he is converted to communism while in a prisoner-of-war camp. Released, he fights bravely against the Nazis and rises to power in the communist hierarchy. There he is finally revolted by the ruthlessness and loss of personal dignity which belong to revoluntionary communism, and is expelled from the party.

At last in a small cell, where he has been placed, his long search for the truth comes to an end. He becomes conscious of what the Christian calls the unmerited grace of God. For the first time he recognizes and acknowledges the presence of God in his life in the world. Gratitude wells up within him. "How was I to give thanks," he says. "What name was I to use? 'God,' I murmured, 'God.'" Then the wonder of God's presence floods over him.

17

"God had been before my eyes from the beginning. . . .
I had needed only to speak His name, which meant to
fear and love Him, to worship Him in love and holy fear."

Sebastian devotes the rest of his life to telling others
of the God who dwells incognito in the heart of all things.
This was his great discovery. His passion became to de-
scribe, interpret, name to others the God whose Spirit
"incognito" is everywhere.

As we accept the inescapable call to mission, we do not
take God into the world. We join him there, for there
in the world is where he belongs.

The Winning of Mass Man

History is determined, more than we realize, by the mass of ordinary people who form the bulk of every society. Christianity began as a movement among average people. Paul says of the early Christians: "Not many of you were wise . . . , not many were powerful, not many were of noble birth" (I Cor. 1:26). The strength of the Methodist revival of the eighteenth century lay in the working classes who responded to the appeal of John Wesley. Communism has changed the course of modern history because it has won the allegiance of the common people of Russia.

There is no future for any movement which fails to stir the masses. Herein lies the chief peril of the Christian church today. The church has largely lost the great segment of the industrialized millions of the world. Appealing in the main to the middle classes and rural communities it no longer knows how to communicate to mass man

19

living in a mass society. With its leadership, both clerical and lay, coming mainly from a certain cultural and economic group, it has lost its ability to quicken the interest of people who rarely read a book and never go to a symphony concert.

Christian history is filled with examples of what happens when the church becomes trapped behind a cultural, economic, or class barrier. When the church has become the concern of a so-called elite, failing to penetrate the mass of people of any area, it is near to extinction.

A modern illustration of what happens comes from Tunisia. During 1964 of the 109 Roman Catholic churches in the former French colony all but 7 were closed. Among them was the massive Cathedral of St. Louis. Some have been turned into museums, some into libraries, some into schools. And why has retreat occurred? Because Roman Catholicism failed to reach the mass of Muslim people who make up Tunisian society.

Nothing is more important to the Christian cause today than recovery amid the great mass of people who live in the cities of the world. No influence with the men of power or wealth, no strength among intellectuals will compensate for losing the masses who inhabit metropolis.

The new society is a mass society. Never before in history have millions of people lived in huddled cities, severed from the soil, with only their labor to sell. Never before have millions of people, by the flick of a switch, been fed by mass ideas, amused by mass entertainment, conditioned by mass suggestion. Never before have millions of people been so completely at the mercy of decisions made by people whom they neither know nor even see. Never before has life been so comfortable, absorbing, exciting as it is in the affluent areas of world life. Never before have the means of living and technology so completely dominated the purposes, the goals of living. And never before has man's immediate physical environment made a spiritual interpretation of life so difficult.

There are features which belong to mass society which profoundly influence the lives of the people and which largely affect the way the mission of Jesus is to be advanced.

John Buchan, once governor-general of Canada, feared the day might come "when life would be lived in the glare of neon lights and the spirit would know no solitude." That day has dawned with the ever expanding mass society.

How hard it is to think of eternal values or to hear the still small voice of God amid the pace and excitement of a modern city. The eyes rarely penetrate beyond the garish city lights to the stars of the heavens. Millions of people whose homes are in sprawling metropolis look constantly on the mean creations of man and can go for years without looking on what God has made. In the overcrowded tenements, the huge apartment houses, the terraced slums, privacy is a luxury and quietness a rarity.

A city is an impersonal place. In country communities people know and are known. Many of us who live in a metropolis do not even know the name of our next-door neighbor or of the family in the apartment above.

Each person in a metropolis becomes like a hard, separate grain of sand on an Australian beach. The weathering of the Hawkesbury River sandstone carries

21

the stone to the ocean where it is churned and broken, soon to become millions of isolated grains of sand without relationship with all the other grains around it. Disintegration of the rock is complete. So the pressures of a mass society destroy community, leaving people isolated and alone.

An impersonal society becomes an irresponsible society. This was seen in three incidents in one week in New York City. A boy got into difficulties off a New York beach. Fifty people watched him drown, and none tried to help. A woman was raped in the entrance of an apartment house. Twenty people looked out of their windows, but did nothing to aid her. Another woman, over a period of a half-hour, was attacked, stabbed, and finally murdered, and in spite of her calls for help none did more than look the other way. No one wanted to become involved.

The French novelist Albert Camus wrote a great novel he called *The Fall* which is about the very problem of noninvolvement in a modern mass city. The setting is Paris. A lawyer, priding himself on his culture and his position, was walking home late across a bridge over the Seine. As he reached the other bank he heard a splash of a body striking the water, and he knew the woman he had just passed was in the river. The lawyer says: "I heard a cry, repeated several times, which was going downstream, then it suddenly ceased. . . . I stood motionless. Then, slowly under the rain, I went away. I informed no one. . . . The next day, and the days following, I didn't read the papers."

Walking, working, living in every metropolis is what David Riesman calls the "lonely crowd." Having spent most of a short lifetime working in the heart of great cities, I realize increasingly how serious is the problem of loneliness. Loneliness has become a deep, modern sickness of soul, bringing far more in its train than is ever realized.

I remember the first funeral I conducted in Sydney, the Australian city where over two million live. The funeral party moved from a small apartment in a multi-storied building. None but the little family stricken in bereavement walked along the corridors to the waiting car. The doors of neighboring apartments were closed; no neighborly concern seemed apparent.

I could only compare it with the coal-mining town from whence I had come. There the sorrow of one seemed to be the sorrow of all. The miners always walked in procession at the funeral of a comrade. I discovered that day the depth of the loneliness of the city.

Out of the impersonal, lonely life of the city comes another feature of its life. It is the anonymous nature of living in metropolis.

It is not an accident that crime is centered in the large cities of the world. Amid the crowded life of London, Paris, Chicago, Sydney, are secreted the crime underworlds and syndicates. Most of us have held to a life of probity in part by the trust and expectation of those around us. It is much harder to walk the white road of conscience when we think no one is looking or listening.

Centered in the cities are the huge financial corporations of the world. In them anonymous action can be taken which, for good or ill, touches countless lives. To dismiss fifty employees whose lives are mere scratchings on a paper is much easier than in smaller businesses where an employer knows his men and the circumstances of their lives. Many a heartless act of injustice is perpetrated in a city precisely because it is done by anonymous, faceless men somewhere in the distance.

Insecurity belongs to the city. Country people, even at a time of recession and depression, can usually scratch some kind of existence from the soil. City people, when unemployment comes, are far more vulnerable. They have only their labor to sell, and there may be no buyers in the marketplace.

Think of some of the elements of insecurity in a city. Without our time payment plans masses of people would never be able to obtain the gadgets and comforts of a mass society. Yet time payments often lead, through over-extension, to a haunting insecurity.

There is the insecurity of sickness, and the dread of the helplessness of old age. Many, in a sense, cannot afford to be sick. The high cost of dying frightens others. Pathetic have been the incidents in my own ministry of people wanting to deposit money for burial, of asking for assurance that, in the hour of passing, amid their loneliness someone will care, someone will do what must be done.

There is another picture to be seen of metropolis. It is the vision of the fascination, excitement, the beauty, the opportunity of the city. In the city are the centers of politics and business, of culture and education, of entertainment and religion. Nowhere in the world are people returning to the country, denuding the cities. As a mighty magnet the metropolis draws people to it.

I can only bear my own testimony. I love the city. I was

24

born in Sydney. I went to school in Sydney. I found my wonderful wife in Sydney. I met God for the first time in the city. I have spent most of my ministry in Sydney. I expect to die in Sydney.

Metropolis will become more attractive, harder to resist. In the cities of the West there will be increasing affluence. More and more people will come to enjoy today's luxuries as necessities. New luxuries will add to the comfort and verve and joy of living.

Of one fact we can be sure. Cities will command an ever greater proportion of the population of the nations. Decentralization has largely failed, and any "back to the country" movement is doomed before it starts.

Metropolis will become megalopolis. Already in America, Washington, D.C. is almost linked to New York and New York to Boston in one huge area of habitation. In Australia, Newcastle, Sydney, Wollongong are destined to become one large megalopolis.

The crucial battle line for the Christian faith runs through metropolis. To fail to win the masses of people living in the cities of the world is to fail. Advance, victory elsewhere cannot compensate for failure on the most important front of all. In the days of Jesus, the New Testament says he had "compassion on the multitude." The test of obedience within the church will be seen in the quality of concern shown by his disciples for the multitudes found in metropolis.

The Christian church is at its weakest today in the great cities of the world. At the center of every metropolis is spiritually a "dead heart," as arid and lifeless as the waterless wilderness in the center of the Australian continent.

In the pleasant residential suburbs the church is outwardly still strong, yet its influence is restricted, for its ministries are carried on far from where the vital decisions affecting the life of society are made. No failure of the church today is so great as its failure to proclaim its witness in power in the midst of metropolis.

Let me illustrate what has happened in the place I know best, in the Australian city of Sydney where 2,500,-000 people who would claim to be nominally Christian live.

The churches have all steadily retreated from the inner belts of the city where the people live in greatest density. The Methodist and Anglican churches hang on longest and, when at last defeat is acknowledged, they have been the last to go. Methodism today, after 150 years of witness in the inner suburbs where 500,000 live, has been reduced to negligible proportions. Today the total Methodist membership of the area is only 3,000 souls.

Roman Catholicism has a better record than Protestantism in the inner areas of most cities. However, it too has no answer to the "soul erosion" which industrialized cities reveal. A. B. Santamaria, the leading Australian Roman Catholic layman, has stated that of every two practicing Roman Catholics who move from rural areas into the cities one is lost to the church.

Life in the inner belts of large cities is antagonistic to worship and the church. The struggle for existence among lower income groups, the harshness of the material environment, overcrowding, all seem to crush and suffocate the life of the spirit.

When all allowance has been made for the effects of

an alien and difficult environment, the failure of the church itself in the inner city stands starkly revealed. The church itself has retreated, abandoning the people.

In the long story of evolution, species which have been unable to adjust to a changed environment have perished. The same fate overtakes human institutions which cannot alter patterns of life and behavior to match changing conditions. The greatest single reason for the collapse of the inner city church is its failure to change with changing circumstances.

The most searching analysis of the failure of the inner city church of recent years has been given by Gibson Winter in his two books *The Suburban Captivity of the Churches* and *New Creation in Metropolis*.

Here is a church. It stood once in a good, even well-to-do residential suburb. It began as a struggling cause when the community was young. The families which made their homes there, with their children about them, worshiped and prayed in the church they loved. Sacrificially they gave, until at last the great day arrived when the lovely, imposing sanctuary was opened. With its auxiliary premises the church for years was thronged, meeting the spiritual needs of the people.

Then the church, like the community around it, began to grow old. The young people in the homes married and moved away. The work among children and young people declined. No longer was the church crowded with people. For those who remained the property now became a liability, its upkeep a burden almost too heavy to bear.

Around the church changes have occurred. The large homes are divided into apartments. Any vacant land has high-density housing built upon it. A new kind of resident appears. There are now more people than ever in the shadow of the church, but it means nothing to them, they had no part in building it.

Within the church there is a stubborn resistence to change. Here the old people cling to one area of life which reflects the cherished past. They even consciously or unconsciously exclude the new people who may be knocking at the church door. As for changing worship or group activities to interest people who follow a different style of life—that is unthinkable. So as the suburb becomes more densely filled with people, the church empties. Soon it is like a piece of rotting driftwood left by a receding tide. At last, after lingering on for years in a largely useless existence, the denomination realizes the only value which remains, its economic value, sells it and uses the money to become established in some new growing suburb. There the process begins again of the birth, youth, mid-years, and growing old of a church.

There is possibly no greater institutional failure in the twentieth century than the failure of the church in the inner city in its local congregational life. Carrying on with a nineteenth-century program in nineteenth-century style buildings, it has come near to extinction at the heart of metropolis.

In the dormitory suburbs of metropolis, the Christian church has written some of its greatest triumphs. There it has gathered people to experience the gospel in great numbers. There it has nurtured the children, served the family, brought the grace of God to men and women for their daily task out in the world.

28

From these suburban churches of the Christian world have come the spiritual momentum, the personal dedication and sacrifice, and the financial resources for the missionary outreach of Christ's cause. Apart from the men who have come from rural areas, the man power for the ministry of the churches has largely been drawn from the congregations of suburbia. The servant agencies of the church have been sustained by these same vital, living Christian cells.

The weakness of the suburban congregation is that its ministry has been in the dormitory situation. It has thus been geographically separated from the centers of business, factory, and professional life. Therefore its ministry has too often been not at the center but at the circumference of life.

When the decline of the church in the inner city is placed with the limits imposed by a dormitory suburb ministry another reason becomes apparent for the loss of the masses in metropolis. The church has appeared irrelevant to the basic struggles of the people and of no importance in relation to the great issues confronting society.

The prophetic church has been all too silent during the twentieth century. The working class masses have looked in vain to the church to give leadership in the struggle for economic justice and have turned to the trade union movement. Minority groups seeking racial justice have gained little leadership from the church. On the immense issues of peace and war and the threat of nuclear destruction the Christian church has been conformist within the national state rather than the prophetic herald of one world living at peace.

29

So masses of people are passing the church by, rejecting it as irrelevant to a modern world. This represents the greatest single failure of the church in the twentieth century.

The Christian church began in the city. In the first century the Christian faith first took root in the great cities of the ancient world: Jerusalem, Corinth, Colossae, Rome. It was in a city, Antioch, where the name Christian was first given to the followers of Jesus. Cities then were of course smaller and different from today. But Corinth, for example, was a city of 500,000 people in the day of Paul. As today, cities were the centers of civilization, the places from which the power of governments, business, educational, and cultural life radiated. And it was in them that Christ won his first victories.

Victory today must again be won within the cities of the world. Christ walks amid the masses in metropolis. From among them he calls to his followers, he calls to all who own his name. There we must join him in obedience.

The Primacy of Proclamation

"Now after John was arrested, Jesus came into Galilee, preaching" (Mark 1:14). Proclamation by preaching was Christ's chosen method. The task of the Christian is to find what God is doing, and to do it with him. Here is the supreme reason why preaching is central to the strategy of mission. "Jesus came preaching."

In the communication of truth, nothing is so powerful as a human personality incandescent with the love and power of God. Unpredictable, wonderful things happen when a man stands up to preach. This has been shown a thousand times through the history of the Christian church. Jesus in Galilee, Peter in Jerusalem, Paul on his missionary journeys, revealed the power of preaching. Every century since has its roll call of preachers whose witness in proclamation God used with power.

Proclamation, preaching today is in eclipse. To read some who write of the mission of the church, it is almost a sin to gather congregations of any size to hear the gospel. The little "house church" is the way forward. The Christian must be "the man who listens" and dare not say with boldness what he believes to be true. Panel discussions on television and radio, where one speaker cancels out another, are the current fashion. Religion must at all costs remain intellectually respectable, so it has become a question mark rather than an answer. Dialogue is "in" and monologue is "out." Woe to the man today who believes he has a commission to say: "Thus saith the Lord!"

It is amazing how much can be written of the Christian strategy of mission without a mention of the centrality of preaching. Therefore, great preaching today is rare. Many ministers have no thought of making effective preaching a goal of their lives. Burning convictions and passionate utterances are conspicuous by their absence from large segments of the Church. So has developed the seeming impotence of the pulpit.

There is nothing more needed today in the mission of the church than the rediscovery of the primacy of proclamation. How can the Christian keep quiet? God is our Heavenly Father, Christ has come, the cross and the resurrection stand as God's mighty acts, the Holy Spirit is at work in human hearts and in history, death is swallowed up in eternal life. With good news like this how can we do other than proclaim it? This is the privilege of the Christian.

On Easter Day this year we held a sunrise service in a drive-in theatre in Sydney. From a high platform before the huge white screen we proclaimed the wonderful message: Christ is risen. As the service came to a close a shadow of sadness passed over my mind and heart. Another Easter Morning was over. I had one less Easter now in which to shout the resurrection story. How can we do other than proclaim such a message?

Gustov Wingren had the right idea: "Christ came that there might be preaching."

The Christian gospel must today be proclaimed in a world where the main battle lines between the gospel and the spirit of the age can be discerned. Unless some huge upheaval such as nuclear war engulfs the world, the contour over which the moral and spiritual struggle will wage in the coming years is becoming clear.

First, a battle line is forming around the uniqueness of Christ. On the mission field of the world, the encounter between Christianity and rival world religions has been known by those on those fields. Now, with the breaking down of distance, rapid world travel, and the interchange of people, men and women are everywhere being forced to measure Christ beside rival world religious leaders and faiths as never before.

On the outskirts of Chicago is a Bahai temple. It symbolizes the appeal of syncretistic religion. There are nine doors in the Bahai temple, each representing one of the great religions of the world. Christianity is there, but merely one of nine doors. The doors all open into the central shrine. The symbolism suggests that one doorway, one religion, is as good as another. All lead into the inner shrine of God's presence.

Bahaism, which is a heretical sect of Islam, makes a subtle appeal to the modern mind. It sounds so rational and tolerant. With Christian truth meaning little to millions, it is easy to sacrifice it and to plead for an amalgam of all religions. It would make living together so much easier—so it is claimed.

Religious syncretism is totally unacceptable to the Christian. The theme of the New Delhi Assembly of the World Council of Churches was prophetic: "Jesus, the Light of the World." Christ, not a light, but the light of men.

With persistence and power the uniqueness of Christ must be proclaimed. It must be a central message of the preacher. Back to the first century we must go, when the early church faced its first encounter with the religions of the day. There was no timidity, no apology, no adjustment. Jesus alone was offered as the hope of the world. "There is salvation in no one else," said Peter. "There is no other name under heaven given among men by which we must be saved" (Acts 4:12).

Second, there is taking shape a sharp conflict between the Christian faith and scientific humanism. The conflict between religion and science is by no means over. The penetration of outer space has in a peculiar way pushed God farther into the distance. It has added to man's pride and self-sufficiency.

So much that God once did, man now seems able to do for himself. Men and women are now in control. Take, for example, a simple illustration seen in a New York subway train. An adoring mother is looking at the hair of her little girl. The color is called "Moon Haze." The caption reads: "Up to now you had to be born with this hair color." Now of course, it comes from a bottle!

34

God, in other words, is supplemented to say the least.

The advance of knowledge of the processes of mind and the development of techniques of psychology and psychiatry have forced God deeper into the recesses of the Soul. Techniques of release seem to be able to do for guilt, for example, what once only repentance and forgiveness could do.

This is a line of argument I can never follow. But that it is heightening the agnosticism, the atheism of many, is undeniable. It has become a vital area of contention in today's world.

For me, far from losing God in outer space, I find him there. With new wonder and adoration I want to fall before the creator, saying, How great thou art! In the soul of man I find nothing has happened which dispenses with God. I echo the words quoted in *Barriers to Christian Belief* by Leonard Griffith: "Nothing has been gleaned from the Milky Way which has made the good life easier or wrong less attractive. There is nothing out there that can warm one heart chilled with loneliness here, or bandage one mind that is bleeding to death from doubt, or forgive one sin that has turned one person prematurely grey."

Third, a Christian battle line is forming around the Christian doctrine of man. What is the nature and destiny of people? What price is to be placed on a man or a woman's life?

The real issue behind racialism concerns the doctrine of man. The rising issue of automation and what it will do to the employment of people will not long remain largely beneath the surface of world attention. War, with nuclear massacre as its inevitable accompaniment, poses

35

the question in its starkest form. How shall human personality be valued?

To the ancient exploitations of men and women, new injustices are being added. There has developed a vast exploitation of the teenager in modern society. Discovering the economic value which the teenage market represents there is to some degree a shameless stimulation of youth which is based on little respect for personality.

There is a new "white slaver" in today's society who exploits women to the utmost. The film industry, the magazine trade without restraint too often degrade womanhood for gain and exploit the loveliness of the human body for profit.

Indeed, the whole world of advertizing raises basic issues as to the right of choice, of rejection of personality. "Brain-washing," saturation propaganda, subliminal advertising pose deep issues for all who care for the integrity of people. We are moving quickly into a world where the Christian estimate of personality, the belief that men and women are the sons and daughters of God, will be a vitally relevant and necessary belief.

Fourth, an intense conflict is joined concerning sexual morality. In western society Christian attitudes and standards on sexual relationships have become accepted as the norm. One man, one woman, married for life, was the unquestioned ideal. Chastity before marriage, fidelity after it, was the accepted way to live. Many of course found it impossible to reach such standards and departed from them, but the standard remained.

Now all is changing. The normal standard has been repudiated so often by so many people, and so publicly by people with some prominence in society, that the standard itself is now being dragged downward.

So an old battle must be refought. The so-called New Morality has raised its hoary head and arguments once again. Now it will be a clear-cut struggle. Contraception has taken away many of the extraneous fears from relationships between men and women. Now God's purpose for people, God's design for marriage and the family, God's laws must become alone the basis for behavior. Now the Christian must proclaim the truth that contraceptives may stop conception, but nothing science can do will give protection from the sorrows sexual license bring on the family or save the individual from the destructive power of unbridled sex. Now the Christian case for sex standards rests on Christ's concern for people. In *Honest to God* John A. T. Robinson says: "Chastity is the expression of caring—of caring, enough."

Fifth, the church must win the battle in some countries and retain it in others to be able with freedom to proclaim a prophetic witness. In communist lands the church is tolerated as long as it remains silent on public issues and thinks and witnesses in the framework of personal religion and an acceptance of the structure and policy of the society in which it lives. In places like South Africa the church suffers restrictions on freely proclaiming its total message on such mass media as the South African radio network. In America and Australia there are heavy social pressures against the pulpit being free to speak as it may or must on such issues as economic practices and international affairs.

With mass media dominating the world of ideas, freedom to criticize, to be nonconformist is obviously in jeopardy. With an affluent society, social criticism is much more difficult to voice. Yet the world needs a church with integrity, freedom, and strength more than ever before. The battle could become intense between a prophetic church and the forces of reaction.

The Christian church has greater intellectual resources than for centuries to plunge to battle. Over the years of this century there has been a tremendous strengthening of the foundations of faith. The Bible today is virtually a new Bible. Gone is the old literalism and in its place has come an understanding of the origin and transmission of the Scriptures which allow the Christian worthily to give an explanation of the faith he holds. After decades of uncertainty, of a liberal extremism which was as distorted as the fundamentalism it tried to replace, the truth and authority of the Bible are emerging with power. Now we are able, to use a concept expressed by Martin Luther, to hear rising out of the many words of the Bible, the Word of God.

During the tumultuous years of the twentieth century, world society has been shaken to its foundations. Amid the turmoil, much that was thought to be true has been swept away. But the Christian faith remains. Christ steps from these years with his insights confirmed and his authority unshaken. In confidence the proclamation can be shouted round the world: Christianity is true.

From a strengthened base, from a period of defense, the time has come for boldness. The world moves quickly into a new era. The Christian thinker must today move ahead of it, giving direction.

The world today needs a "theology of growth" rather than a "theology of crisis." Out of a "sick" Europe has come almost a "sick" theology. From 1900 to 1950, amid a deepening world crisis, a theology matching world need was required.

Now mankind marches onward. Now Christian direction and discipline are needed to guide and chasten the bounding, forward-looking energy of masses of the people. Affluence, making possible a good life in terms of material comfort, once beyond mankind's wildest dreams, is here. Former colonies by the dozen become young, free, confident nations determined to fashion their own lives. New perils, new idolatries appear, and the world cries out for Christian intellectual leadership which will guide it past the pitfalls on the way to the new day of plenty.

Perhaps I reflect the optimism, the pleasantness of Australia, where we have a limited past and a mighty future. Perhaps as a consequence I am minimizing the tragic overtones undoubtedly always present amid unredeemed humanity. Yet, I want a theology which tells of fulfillment. I want to hold aloft a Christ who said, as translated by James Moffatt: "I am come that you may have life and have it to the full."

The time has come to proclaim to the world a mature, adult God who works with us in the world he has not only made but is in the process of making. In a world which Dietrich Bonhoeffer claims at last has "come of age," the preacher, in the name of Christ, can offer a grown-up God.

Let us be quite frank; mankind has too often been given the picture of a God who treats people as children. Why we even use the phrase in speaking and praying before mature congregations, "the children of God"!

Similarly, God has been presented as one who seems to want to keep his creatures in a dependent, subservient state. The metaphors used are of obedient subjects in the presence of a king, of humble suppliants before a lord, of sheep—docile, brainless sheep—meekly following a shepherd. When you think of it, no wonder grown men and women rebel at the infantile regression religious faith seems to require.

God is likewise the God who appeals to us in our weakness and comes to us almost exclusively in the hour of crisis. Somehow the vision of a God who rejoices in our strength and meets us in the full tide of our success, passes us by.

There is another God in the pages of the New Testament. When Jesus uses the word "Father," it is impressive, strong. It is a son of mature years who has become a companion to his father, sharing his mind and purposes, who is speaking. "My Father is working still, and I am working," said Jesus (John 5:17). This is not the language of a little boy dependent on his "daddy." This is father and son in partnership together, responsibly sharing a common task.

God is calling to us, his grown, mature sons and daughters to cooperate with him in fashioning to completion his unfinished world. He points us to a natural environment to be harnessed to the service of humanity. He challenges us to make of the tribes of the earth one universal family living at peace. He inspires us to subdue the thus far unsubduable—man's atomic heart. He directs us to a universe of unbelievable dimensions and bids us explore the vastness of outer space. He sends us to the ends of the earth to tell the good news that Christ has come and shows us a world to be redeemed.

> This, this is the God we adore,
> Our faithful, unchangeable Friend;
> Whose love is as great as His power,
> And neither knows measure nor end.

This is the message I want to proclaim. It is a noble, stupendous message worthy of God and worthy of man. Because of it I am ready to obey the words of Jesus: "Go into all the world and preach the Gospel to the whole creation" (Mark 16:15).

Worship in the World

Worship is a great instrument for mission. At worship in churches round the world more people encounter the Christian gospel than in any other way. Worship that is full of vitality and relevance sustains and expands the mission of Jesus.

What has gone wrong with worship in many churches? Why do so many people pass the church by Sunday after Sunday? Perhaps Walter Lippmann has given the answer in *Preface to Morals*. "Surely the most important reason is that they are not so certain that they are going to meet God when they go to church."

The great need today is to let the world into worship, and to thrust worship out into the world. Something has gone wrong with the act of worship in many churches. Detached, lifeless, dull, it no longer seems relevant to life. So, isolated from the pulsing stream of life, it has become a little backwater experience, the private interest of the few instead of the eager concern of all.

Worship has also become an end in itself. Far from being a time for renewal and a recovery of a sense of direction for daily living it has become a passive hour which has led to a worshiper being called "a church-goer." By becoming an end in itself worship has lost primary meaning and purpose and as a consequence has ceased to interest masses of people who need it.

A great price is being paid today for making religion a separate activity carried on in the main on a special day in a sacred, peculiar building, led by a separated priesthood. As a result, religion has become a specialist interest for part of life rather than a spirit to permeate all life.

Dietrich Bonhoeffer put his finger right on the central need of the church when he pleaded for a "religionless Christianity." The fight that lies ahead is to place the Christian faith at the very heart of life and civilization.

If the world is to be rid of religion as a separatist, specialist activity, anything which gives to it the image of a separate cult must become suspect. The back-to-front collars of ministers and priests, the black habits of nuns, the gaudy vestments and flowing robes of church leaders have become a liability to all who seek the remarriage of religion and life. The intoning voice of the sanctuary, a carry-over from the days before public address and amplification systems, has become a meaningless affectation. Heavy liturgical services expressed in a language nobody uses, accompanied by a musical score few understand, become religious exercises with no meaning beyond themselves.

The time has come to offer people the opportunity of worship outside so-called sacred buildings. For millions now are as uneasy and embarrassed to enter the peculiarly-shaped building we call a church as I would be ill at ease and awkward in a shearing shed or an electrical powerhouse.

From 1908 to 1964 the Central Methodist Mission in Sydney has conducted worship in a theatre. Then its theatre, the Lyceum, was destroyed by fire. At once some people said, Now we can build again and build a beautiful cathedral for Methodism in the heart of Sydney. Our answer was, No, we shall rebuild a theatre.

From the ashes there has arisen, to the glory of God, a theatre. Why? Because we have made an important discovery over these years. There are countless Australians who will enter a theatre, a "non-sacred" building, who would never cross the porch of a church. Over all the years of the history of the Lyceum, large audiences have assembled for what is Australia's largest Sunday night congregation. It is not unrelated to the "religionless Christianity" found within its walls. So we knew if we were to build for the church we would build a church; if we were to build for the world, it must be a theatre.

One Sunday night just before the fire, we had a fine soloist in the evening act of worship. When he finished, one man, not exactly dressed as are most worshipers, began to clap with enthusiasm. Slowly he subsided, for he realized he was the only one applauding. At first I was taken aback, for though a theatre, this was not our practice. Then came the answer: Isn't it wonderful we have at least one man at church tonight who doesn't know it is not usual to clap at worship!

Worship in the world demands far more than offering worship, at least at times in a worldly building. It means designing worship so that it does sound as if it belongs to the twentieth century.

The first battle to be won is to show in worship that the Christian faith is relevant to the life people must live in today's world. This is not easy. Jesus, of course, lived long before the emergence of modern, industrialized mass society. His thought forms were fashioned by a rural environment. Hence he used the language of the countryside—sheep and shepherds, fields and cattle, the birds of the air, the boats of fishermen, the pursuits of the simple home of the first century.

Now, all is changed. Most people look on paved streets and sight not the stars but the glare of neon lights. None has ever seen a shepherd. Ideas live perpetually amid the concepts pumped out by mass entertainment and the environment of the machine. So the language of the Bible and of the hymns and prayers of the church seem part of yesterday, rather than today.

How near, for example, are the pastoral prayers of worship to the life of the people. Take one example. Time payments have created a whole series of new anxieties for modern people. A glimpse into this world of debt and of fear of repossession is given by the playwright Arthur Miller in "Death of a Salesman."

Willy Loman says, "Once in my life I'd like to own something outright before it's broken! I'm always in a race with the junkyard. I just finished paying for the car and it's on its last legs. . . . They time those things. They time them so when you finally paid for them, they're used up."

Amid the joys and sorrows of time payments most of the working class in western society perpetually live. How often have you heard this anxiety mentioned at prayer in a church?

Worship must ever be an engagement with life at a deeper level, not an act of detachment from it. Yet it is at this point our concepts are often wrong.

Where do we most expect to encounter God? Many would answer: as we draw back into quietness. We repeat the line, "Man is nearer God's heart in a garden than anywhere else on earth." This incidentally deserves Russell Maltby's comment that it is just not true—"unless it be the Garden of Gethsemane."

If we examine worship we will notice how often we go wrong. How often have we heard the prayer: "We thank thee, O God, for this time when we can draw aside and be with thee!"

My experience has been different. God has been nearest in my experience when I have been most involved in the struggle of living. I can understand the meaning of the story in the Old Testament when three young men were thrown into the furnace set up on the plains of Dura by King Nebuchadnezzar. A surprised king said, "Did we not cast three men bound into the fire? But I see four men loose, walking in the midst of the fire . . . and the appearance of the fourth is like a son of the gods" (Dan. 3: 24-25).

It is in the furnace the presence of God is known. It

is in the moment, not of detachment, but involvement with life that God comes near. As John A. T. Robinson says: "Prayer is . . . to expect to meet God in the way, not to turn aside from the way." And again: "It is certainly not that disengagement is unnecessary, but that the pentecostal point, as it were, is in the engagement."

Worship and prayer, must then be a point of engagement with life. Only if there is a deeper penetration into life amid worship can it be real. It must be worship in the world.

In the design of public worship two facts must be taken strongly into account. One is that masses of people have no experience of worship. The other is that friendliness, warmth, joy, simplicity are needed in worship for people who live in a mass society.

The modern church has forgotten the wisdom of the early church. In the first Christian century there were two types of worship. One act of worship was designed for baptized Christians. Central to it was the "breaking of bread." A second form of worship was for the pagan. It was designed as a meeting place between the Christian and the non-Christian. It made no assumptions; it tried to start where he was.

Worship in the modern church too often assumes all who attend are Christian believers. It is usually designed *by* an ingroup *for* an ingroup. It fails therefore as an act of mission and expresses no evangelical purpose. To many it appears to be a semisecret rite, the privilege of the initiated.

There are few greater needs in the modern church than to find ways of designing worship for mission. In Australia and England there are often, especially in the center of cities and in industrial communities, large Sunday night acts of worship. Morning and evening worship come to express a different purpose. "We preach to the saints in the morning and the sinners at night," said one famous British preacher. There was truth in the comment. With the decline and death of Sunday night worship as in most places in America it is worship with an evangelical purpose that has suffered. In America it is the sinners who are missing out.

Recently on a Sunday in New York, having preached in the morning, I dearly wanted to worship somewhere on the Sunday night. I searched the religious advertisements of *The New York Times* in vain. After dinner I walked up Broadway. Theatre lights were blazing, many shops were open, the streets were thronged. But the church offered no place for worship in Manhattan that night.

What an opportunity faces the modern church in metropolis to design worship on a Sunday night, not for Christians, but for the near-pagans of our time. In one act a congregation could be led on mission. It could lead again to a rediscovery of worship as an evangelical experience.

Worship with the purpose of mission would be very different. The plain fact is that many acts of worship today completely fail to communicate with all but five per cent of the population. Church music, chosen and presented by developed classical musicians, only speaks to the "symphony-concert" mentality of the few. Classical forms of liturgical worship are just incomprehensible to

48

the non-Christian masses, the formality, the properness merely alienating them.

The so-called liturgical revival of the present-day church could be widening the gulf between the church and the masses. It is not more or different but less ritual that is required. Worship needs not more formality but more spontaneity, not added restraint and austerity but increased joy and enthusiasm, not coldness and distance but intimacy and warmth. At the very hour when the church should be moving out to those beyond its reach, it is retreating within itself, multiplying the detail of liturgy.

For more than half my ministry I was in bondage to what is classical and supposedly proper in worship. Fearful of seeming to cheapen worship, I made it stiff and cold. Then came deliverance. I saw simplicity, directness in style of worship, readily communicated to people in today's society. I discovered how important it is to import even a "folksy" element into worship. I set out to allow for spontaneity and the freedom of the spirit. I found it much harder to prepare for an extempore prayer than to read one out of a book. I learned how much planning is necessary to give lonely people a sense of belonging and to seek warmth and joy in the presence of God. In other words I have learned another way whereby people may catch a glimpse of the Lord high and lifted up.

Many changes would appear in conventional worship if we really learned to communicate through worship in the modern idiom. The movement, the pace, the music, the appearance of worship would all be reexamined. Out of it could come worship not for yesterday but today.

49

How limited has been our use of music in worship. Why are we in bondage to the church organ? "Modern young people no longer 'hear' the diapason stop of an organ," a brilliant young musician said recently to me. "They are used to the sharper tones of the saxaphone and the guitar." God does speak through the downbeat rhythm of a band no less than the steady four-beat bar of a conventional organ.

Theology, and sound theology at that, can be set to swing music. Fast-beat hymns can transfer an act of worship from dullness to vitality. I know, because I have tried it. Some of the most thrilling acts of worship in recent years in our theatre in Sydney have had introduced into them gospel in rhythm.

How important is the pace of worship. People are used to split-second timing in entertainment and on television. They attend church and are irritated beyond measure by the slowness and raggedness of all that happens. Ministers read whole verses of hymns and organists play the lot again as introduction as though people are illiterate. Then, at last, the congregation begins. Pauses between items, slow-talking ministers make not for godliness but annoyance.

Worship in the world means using the idiom of the world. In this sense the need of the church is worldly worship.

"The end of worship—the beginning of service." After the word "Benediction" on our printed order of service in Sydney, this sentence appears.

Strange, is it not, that we call an act of worship a "service"? It is surely a confusion of ideas. It is from worship flows the service of God. Worship is renewal for service. Worship must flow out into the world through the service of the worshiper of God and man or it ceases to be true worship. As Elton Trueblood says in *The Company of the Committed:* "The Company of Jesus is not people streaming to a shrine; and it is not people making up an audience for a speaker; it is laborers engaged in the harvesting task of reaching their perplexed and seeking brethren with something so vital that, if it is received, it will change their lives."

Jesus found it necessary in his day to let religion loose in the world. Then, too, it had become the private interest of the few. The symbol of that release is expressed in Matthew's report of what happened as Christ died on the cross. "And behold, the curtain of the temple was torn in two, from top to bottom" (Matt. 27:51). At that moment profane eyes gazed on the holy of holies. In Jesus religion and life became mixed up together.

The wheel has moved almost full cycle. Once again it is necessary for "the curtain of the temple to be torn in two, from top to bottom."

Christ amid the Lonely Crowd

A revolution is engulfing the neighborhood congregation and the suburban church. The relevance of churches set amid dormitory housing is up for question. The wisdom of sinking vast sums of money in places of worship which by their nature can only be used a few hours a week is being examined afresh. The program, the structure of every Christian congregation is under review. Since the New Delhi Assembly of the World Council of Churches began its study of "The Missionary Structure of the Congregation," a fundamental issue has arisen: What is the missionary function of every local congregation of Christians?

Since the Middle Ages the Christian church has become established amid the homes of the people in towns and cities. And what a saga of achievement has been written. Relevant to the needs of the people, offering pastoral care, a teaching ministry, and Christian fellowship, the strength of the church has become expressed in the neighborhood church. Out of these thousands of churches have moved tens of thousands of Christians to bear their witness in homes of piety and in vocational activity. So great a triumph could not have been recorded if these neighborhood congregations had not been fulfilling the will of God, or meeting real needs among the people. Far from the local parish congregation being popular because it is irrelevant, it could be it is popular because it supplies a necessary ministry.

The day of the neighborhood church is by no means over. The parish congregation will continue to be the strength of the church. Nothing has occurred which makes any less necessary the parish minister offering opportunities of worship, nurture, fellowship, and service to the families and homes of the people.

Social trends could easily move into reverse in the years ahead, increasing again the centrality of the home in the life of the people. Television has already given a new point of gravity within the family circle. Automation, with an inevitable, consequent increase of leisure will add to the hours men and women can potentially spend in the home in the dormitory suburb.

The home, the family, the residential suburb form a part, and a large part of society's life. This makes extreme the point of view of young people in Brazil as quoted by Colin Williams in his book *What in the World*. They say: "The more we participate in the life of the congregation, the more alienated we become from the real world in which we are convinced God has called us to live and

53

witness." Surely family life and dormitory suburbs are part of the real world.

The great error of many a neighborhood church is not in what it is doing, but in the fact that it does not go far enough. Now masses of people live permanently beyond the conventional ministries of the church. They never will be reached by congregations who make no effort to turn eyes outward to them. On many of the effective present ministries of neighborhood churches new missionary structures must be built.

In apartment house areas, in the inner belts of cities, amid the thousands who make up the lower economic groups of metropolis, revolutionary planning is needed. It is in these areas especially that existent congregations must go on mission. Among specific groups of people with special needs, particular patterns of mission are essential.

Many, many are the experiments in new congregational patterns that are required. From them will come insights as to how to serve in the nondomitory situations of today's complex society. Harvey Cox states the situation in his book *The Secular City*. "We are moving into a stage in which we will need a widely differentiated range of different types of church organization to engage a society which is becoming differentiated at an accelerated rate. Not only will future forms of church life be differentiated and specialized, they must also be flexible and disposable, ready in their turn to give way to ever newer forms."

Recently, on a pleasant summer evening, I visited several of the social clubs which since the Second World War have spread across New South Wales. Beyond attractive entrance foyers I found hundreds of people in-

formally eating, drinking, playing games, chatting together, dancing. In well-lit rooms and lounges the people
were making the most of the new leisure of modern
society.

How has the club come into being and what keeps it
going? Certainly the presence of the gambling machine
and the liquor bar have provided almost unlimited money
to club boards of management for the building of their
palatial premises. But why, I kept asking, have registered
clubs increased from 240 to 1,400 in the state in twelve
years?

There is but one answer. The club is filling a vacuum
that has developed in society. Amid the impersonal, lonely
city it provides a place for meeting. For lonely people, tir-
ing of the isolated experience which television watching
in the home represents, the club is meeting real needs.

On the twenty mile journey around Sydney, which was
part of my "club crawl," I passed scores of churches. On
that evening every one of them was dark, closed and
deserted. Many of the churches and their auxiliary
premises stood on street corners, commanding magnificent
sites. But none, on that night, seemingly had anything to
offer a fellowship starved community.

In my state, I am convinced that the coming of the
clubs represents a judgment on the churches. Although
the possessors of that precious gift called Christian fellowship, they have neither seen its relevance nor learned
how to express it. Another crucial opportunity to meet
the needs of people in today's world has been largely
missed.

Loneliness is a serious modern sickness of soul. David

Reisman has really captured the truth in a phrase when he called his book *The Lonely Crowd*. It is amid the crowds which throng metropolis that loneliness is so acute. In country districts everyone knows everyone; in the city we scarcely even know the name of our next-door neighbor or the people in the apartments above or below. So rootless, isolated, community-less people abound.

The depth of loneliness which exists in a modern city is shown by facts surrounding the high incidence of suicide today. We have learned in Sydney in our suicide prevention work that the largest number of calls comes from the inner city, from a circle with a three to four mile radius from the center of the city. The Mental Health Research Group in England declares the same phenomenon appears elsewhere: "Research in London, Chicago and elsewhere has confirmed unusually high rates in the shifting lodging house communities that typically surround the railway stations in large towns; especially among people living alone."

Every neighborhood church has at hand an immediate strategy for mission in the provision of fellowship, in placing Christ amid the lonely crowd. For the church to put its properties back into circulation, to open its doors not one but seven days a week, to design its programs to offer fellowship would transform many a local situation.

It is salutatory to remember the experience of the church in the first three centuries of its history. Over those years the church was unable to own property. Yet over those three hundred years the fellowship of Christains held and the church marched forward. What a quality of fellowship around the risen Christ there must have been.

I remember realizing something of what that first-century fellowship must have been, in my first visit to Rome. Just at dusk one evening I stood before that rude cross which stands in the Coliseum marking the point from which the early Christians were brought out of the cells to face the lions in the arena. As I looked at the moldering tiers on which the hostile crowds sat, and thought of the might of the Roman Caesar and his empire, I wondered however those early Christians found the courage to die.

The next day I went down into the catacombs outside the city. I saw there the tunnels where the early Christians gathered to worship the risen Christ. There were the mounds of earth, where the tunnels widened, on which the bread and wine were spread.

Suddenly the link between the cross in the arena and tha catacombs became clear. The early Christians went out to die, not alone, but in the power of the fellowship in which they had shared worship together. From Christian fellowship came the power to witness, and by fellowship they were made strong.

Christian fellowship can be of two kinds. It can have as its purpose the nurture of Christians. In the unity which a common acceptance of Christ gives, it can be the atmosphere in which people grow to a deeper maturity.

Fellowship can be used with an evangelical purpose. It then becomes the gathering together of people who accept no Christian commitment. With a group of dedicated Christians at its center this kind of fellowship can be the place of encounter, of dialogue, of mission. Through the gift of fellowship to the isolated and the lonely, the servant church meets the needs of the people.

At the Central Methodist Mission in Sydney we have developed a policy through which we offer fellowship to all who will come. Through specially designed buildings, loosely organized activities and a dynamic group program, a major thrust into the community has taken shape.

Buildings designed for fellowship are a basic need. They need not be lavish, large, or costly. They must suggest open-hearted hospitality, warmth, intimacy. Most churches spend their money on two large buildings—the worship sanctuary and a public hall—to accommodate crowds. Every Church needs auxiliary premises in which, through smaller groups, fellowship may develop.

We have a fellowship center in which we have learned certain facilities are basic. At the top of the list I would place facilities for eating together. Jesus knew what he was doing when he made a fellowship meal, the Lord's Supper, central. Real fellowship can develop in eating together. So we have our restaurant and a snack bar, open seven days a week.

Lounges, game rooms, club facilities, reading room, library, a teenage "rumpus room" where the jukebox plays and youth can plan its own life, are essential. Inviting foyers and bright lighting are part of the attractiveness. A fellowship center designed to suggest that friendship almost comes out of the walls can become a tremendous physical instrument in the hands of God.

Loosely structured programs are essential. In a highly

58

organized society people shrink from being organized in their leisure hours. Herein lies the appeal of the "coffee house" evangelism which has become a feature in so many places, especially on and near university campuses.

Our fellowship center gathers hundreds of people weekly just to eat and drink together. Meal hours are the busy hours. Every Wednesday night is "folk lounge" night, as pleasant folk music is offered as people sit and eat. Through it all a friendship core of Christians make their links with those who gather, seeking an entry into their lives, entering into dialogue with them in thought and experience.

Beyond the freedom of unorganized fellowship are the groups made up of people of common interests. The names of some of the groups indicate their nature—the Business Women's Group, the Young Adults, the Senior Fellowship, the International Youth Club, the Couples' Club, the Young Marrieds.

Perhaps the most significant group of all is Crossways. It is a men's luncheon group made up of a membership that is one third professional men, one third businessmen, and one third trade union leaders. In Australia many trade union leaders rarely sit down with people from the business and professional classes. At Crossways there is encounter, fellowship, even reconciliation. Why, some trade unionists of the "right" and "left" meet almost only at Crossways.

We have made an important discovery in group work. Most of us within the church are obsessed with numbers. We have sought to increase the size of the groups within our fellowship program. Try as we will, we cannot seem to lift them above the forty to fifty mark. Then it suddenly struck us. Is this the number beyond which a group becomes a crowd? Is the task then to multiply groups rather than to seek larger membership of existent groups?

The need of people is to be able to say that lovely little phrase, I belong. It can only be said by people who are not lost in a crowd, but are set within a fellowship community small enough for each one to count. The church in which people of all types can meet, worship, think, enjoy leisure together, is bringing to a mass society the vital service of group therapy.

There are many experiments beginning to emerge around the world showing how congregations can go on mission. "Coffee house" evangelism has become almost a convention in America. The Potter House in Washington and The Door in Chicago have many emulating their work, as backed by Christian commitment and prayer, encounter with those beyond the more regular ministries of the church is sought. "The Night Pastor" moving through the nightclub district of Chicago with his office open at offbeat hours to all who may come, is the church going not only to those who need it, but to those who may need it most. There are operating in Great Britain striking experiments in youth club evangelism. The multilingual church in Carlton, Melbourne, is a brave attempt to conquer the speech barrier amid the many European migrants flooding into Australia.

Let it be said it is proving relatively easy to gather people into youth clubs and coffee shops. It is the next step which is difficult. How are people to find their way from the pleasant and friendly atmosphere of a coffee shop to an acceptance of Christian truth and ethic and the life of obedience and growth toward Christian maturity in Jesus Christ.

There are those who are content to be a "presence" expressing Christian concern among the people. Anything under the sun can be introduced in conversation except religion. Fearful of giving offense, the serving with graciousness of a cup of coffee is enough.

Here, it seems to me, is reappearing under a new guise the worst elements of the old theological liberalism. The essence of the gospel, the Kerygma means nothing. Ethical convictions which stem from theological truth are of little account. In some vague and insubstantial way it is sufficient to communicate a sense of Christian concern. Little or no attempt is made to graft men and women into the body of Christ, the church.

There is a guidance which comes from the New Testament. There the name of Jesus was an offense and the cross a scandal. Yet sooner or later the name was mentioned. Peter and John, for example, at the porch of the temple in Jerusalem said to a crippled man: "I have no silver and gold, but I give you what I have; in the name of Jesus Christ of Nazareth, walk" (Acts 3:6).

In the end the name—of God, of Christ, of the Holy Spirit, of the church—must be spoken. How else shall the true missionary purpose of the dedicated congregation or of the serving, witnessing Christian be finally fulfilled? Later rather than sooner, no doubt, but somewhere not vague influence but a winning to a specific commitment must be achieved. Nothing less justifies the endless man-hours spent in offering service and fellowship to those beyond. A congregation on mission has no alternative but to obey with wisdom the charge of the psalmist: "Let the redeemed of the Lord say so" (Ps. 107:2).

Faith for the Teenager

"The Church, it seems to me, is very good at casting the net on the wrong side of the ship." So said a woman who was standing outside Teenage Cabaret in Sydney, watching the hundreds of young people streaming into the city streets.

A few weeks earlier this woman called us, concerned about her daughter who had rebelled against the church. She asked whether she could bring her daughter to our youth center, in the hope it might give to a teenager in rebellion a different image of the church.

A criticism of Teenage Cabaret by a friend set her thinking. She happened to read the story of the post-resurrection appearance of Jesus in Galilee. There he found his disciples disappointed at fishing all night for nothing. "Cast the net on the right side of the boat, and you will find some," he said. "So they cast it, and now they were not able to haul it in, for the quantity of fish" (John 21: 6-7).

Seeing some relevance between the story in John's Gospel and the moden youth work of the church, she made her judgment. As with many of us, she was concerned about the failure of the church to communicate to the modern teenager.

The world today has discovered, or should we say created, the teenager as a special group in the community, with particular needs and problems. Young people walking that fateful passage between childhood and adulthood do form a group apart needing understanding and patience.

One fact stands out clearly. It is that the teenage years are the years of decision. Most of the important choices which affect people for the rest of their lives are made in these years. Choice of career and marriage partner, political sympathies and a philosophy of living come for many at this time. It is the great time of religious decision when a commitment to Christ as Savior and Lord can be made which lasts for life.

The first seven years of a child's life are often quoted as being all-important in the formation of attitudes and behavior. I have learned rather of the significance of adolescence. It is in these years the child moves out of a sheltered life and must cope with the inner drives of sex and the outer pressures of higher education or the world of work. It is the teenager, with limited knowledge and an immaturity of emotions, who is suddenly expected to act as responsibly as a fully developed body would seem to imply. In these years comes the great opportunity to present the claims of the living Christ.

How poorly the Christian church has responded to the challenge of the teenager. Many neighborhood churches have splendid programs for young people already linked to the church through family affiliations. Few churches do anything to reach the vast army of teenagers in western society who live perpetually beyond the ministry of the church. So the church today registers another failure.

The effectiveness of the church depends more than is realized on what happens to the teenager. A phenomenon of population trends is the growing percentage of adolescents in the total population.

Australian figures are startling. The following is the actual and projected picture of the percentage of young people of the eleven to nineteen age group in the total population.

Year	Ages from 11 to 19	Total Population	Percentage of 11 to 19 years in total population
1953	1,232,913	8,829,465	13.96
1958	1,596,610	9,846,140	16.22
1963	1,970,012	10,916,249	18.05
1966	2,126,500	11,595,200	18.34
1971	2,280,400	12,865,700	17.73
1976	2,492,500	14,354,400	17.36
1986	3,268,300	17,806,800	18.35

These figures are based on the assumption that the birthrate will remain at the 1965 level and that migration will continue at what is regarded as a minimum rate.

All this means that the Christian church will go on

carrying a huge responsibility for youth and that it faces an unparalleled opportunity to win them for Christ.

My own teenage boys persuaded me to go with them to hear the English entertainment troupe called "The Beatles." It was a night to remember. Some 17,000 teenagers thronged the Sydney Stadium. I tried to analyze what was happening as I listened and watched the performers—the squealing effectively drowned the music of the band. I watched the unrestrained excitement, the girls throwing "jelly-babies" at the young men, exclaiming, "Mine touched him, mine touched him," if the aim was accurate. I sensed the rhythm, the abandon as I grappled for explanations.

On the way home I asked our youngest boy why it was "mighty." "Oh," he said, "you can let yourself go." I asked a teenage girl I knew, "Why do you stomp and squeal?" "You get things out of your system when you squeal."

A little light began to dawn. Teenagers grappling with growing emotions, awakening sex desire, trying to handle social relationships, scarcely know how to handle life. Moving out into the world of work with its limitations and frustrations, pressures build up within. Rebelling against adults who, they feel, have little understanding of them, they yearn for freedom from authority. By rocking and rolling, squealing and stomping, they find release.

I have come to the conclusion that there is a pathetic "lostness" about millions of teenagers in western society. Many can almost be described as "detribalized white people." In primitive communities where culture contact has been rapid and powerful, there often emerges the "detribalized native." With his own faith in the spirit world, his tribal culture torn down, he becomes a person lost between two worlds.

Hosts of teenagers today reveal this kind of "lostness." They are separated by three or four generations from a living religious faith. They have no Christian memories any more. It is useless to appeal to Christian faith and ethics. They have little by which to interpret what is communicated to them. Many young people today have no faith to live by, no cause to live for, and no leader worth the following.

On moral questions, most of the signposts are down. This is especially true of the whole area of sex ethics. As one young American said to me during a Religious Emphasis Week: "I want to do what is right, but how do you know what is right to do?" Before such confusion it is amazing to me that modern youth has shown such moral balance. Apart from the small minority of antisocial delinquents there is something morally wholesome and resilient about today's generation of young people.

It is in this context that the mission of the church to youth must be undertaken. Let it be recognized that at least in Australia the church has the oldest and largest youth activities in the country. There is a long background of experience and much voluntary, dedicated leadership upon which it can draw.

A church which goes on mission amid today's teenagers must assume that the gulf between young people and the Christian faith is wide and deep. It is far too wide to be crossed in one leap.

With this assumption we have set out in youth planning

to create a series of clubs and programs which would be as stepping stones across a river. On Saturday night we have Teenage Cabaret, which strives to begin where the young people are. On Friday is the Young Sydney Club. It has a more developed Christian content. Sunday brings the Youth Fellowship Hour following evening worship, which moves on a deeper level again.

The aim of our youth work is to bring teenagers to a moment of definite personal commitment to Jesus Christ. When this moment comes, two further youth activities are available. There is a youth section in the weekly College for Christians. Through it they become part of a Christian education program. They may join Young Life Liners, where the emphasis is on witness and service.

The most controversial and successful element within the total youth policy of the Central Methodist Mission is Teenage Cabaret. By it we make a continuing contact with the nonchurch youth of the city; through it we have learned most of what we know about the teenager.

Teenage Cabaret emerged after months of experimenting. Concerned that we were failing in youth outreach, we first set out to listen and understand. Groups of Christian young people visited the milk bars and other meeting places for youth in the city. From what was learned came our conviction that no youth program would succeed which did not start where the young people were in interest and attitude.

There was at hand a ready-made starting point in the music and dancing interest of youth. We listened to their music and watched their habits. While recognizing dangers in both, we decided a Christian church could use them and build on them.

For six months we tried one form of presentation after another. Gradually we advanced in understanding of what might succeed and in sureness of touch toward the teenagers. We drew for guidance, where possible, on a similar venture in Brisbane, Australia, led by the Reverend Arthur Preston. We adopted the name he used, Teenage Cabaret.

With a fanfare of publicity, Teenage Cabaret was launched. On the opening night hundreds of teenagers thronged the street waiting for the doors to open. Within half an hour the building was jammed to capacity and hundreds were turned away. On that night Teenage Cabaret was born. Now, as I write, five years later, still the crowds come, still almost every Saturday night of the year the "House Full" sign goes up, still hundreds cannot get in.

Now, what happens at Teenage Cabaret? At 6 o'clock each Saturday the Christian core of young people meets for a prayer meeting. This is vital. I have not before in my ministry been given such observable evidence of the effects of prayer. If we have a good prayer meeting it strengthens the whole night; if we have a thin prayer meeting the night becomes ragged and shallow. At the prayer meeting we brief our young people, giving training in how to make friends with non-Christian youth.

At 7 o'clock the doors to Teenage Cabaret open. After paying an entrance fee the young people stream in where the five-piece band is playing. The program is loosely organized until 8 P.M., when the first floor show is presented. This floor show is merely teenage artists singing on the stage to the music of the band.

For the fourth spot of the night, the main one, we are able to get one of the named stars who have records on the Australian market. The star item of the night is held at 9:15 P.M., and for that we ask all the young people to come down from the other two floors and stand together in the packed auditorium.

Immediately following this main entertainment item, there steps on to the stage a Gospel Rhythm Choir. It introduces the "Christian Floor Show" by singing a Christian hymn or a Negro spiritual in fast rhythm.

A seven-minute message follows. For me it is the toughest speaking assignment of any week. Attention must be won and held. Directness of speech, special care in vocabulary, strength and authority in approach are all needed. Always there must be the assumption that it is a raw missionary situation, where spiritually illiterate people are possibly hearing the gospel almost for the first time.

Throughout the night a "friendship core" of young people committed to the Christian way move among all who come, entering into dialogue, coming to know them. The minister on duty is available during the evening. Following the "Christian Floor Show" he stands outside the small chapel and teenagers come, talking, telling their problems, inquiring about the Christian faith.

Nothing has proved more difficult than verbal communication. To begin with, our whole Christian vocabulary is largely meaningless. Biblical references are wasted, even the best known stories of the Bible such as the parables of the good Samaritan and the prodigal son must be told

as new stories, and the impact is as on people who hear
them for the first time. We have learned however the
tremendous thrust and power of an easily understood
Bible sentence when it is relevant or sums up the message
being given.

There is many a shock. The crowd seems to hear something different from what is said or intended. The
laughter, the noisy reaction often come at unexpected
moments. There are some words we try to avoid for
they always bring a snicker or a guffaw. For example,
when I say "love" they hear "sex," when I use the word
"spirit" they hear "liquor." One of the saddest discoveries
is how often a sex symbol seems to be seen in what is
said. The exploitation by commercial interests of the
natural sex interest of youth is causing many to live perpetually in a sex thought-world.

One of the best hearings ever gained was when "The
Beatles" were in town. That Saturday I know I was able
to start where they were.

"I went to see the Beatles last night," I began, and drew
squeals and whistles. "I know now why you like to let
yourself go, you get things out of the system: frustrations,
disappointments, pent-up emotions. But you know, there
are some things you cannot get rid of by shouting and
stomping. Guilt, for example, and jealousy, bitterness, and
hatred. Fear, too, lies deeper than a squeal. This is why
you need Christ. His forgiveness gets rid of guilt. His love
sets us free from bitterness and hatred. His teaching about
God casts out fear. This is why Jesus means so much. He
is 'the most.' "

We have learned how to handle large crowds of teenagers. The modern "downbeat" music, played with the excessive volume liked by teenagers, must not continue over too long a period of time. It pounds into the mind, deadening the higher levels of personality almost like a drug. The danger is then that the youngsters slip down the gradient to mass emotion, bringing with it the peril of disorder and fighting. So we ring the changes throughout the night with pauses, by presenting at intervals softer music with a different rhythm. Above all we need the "Christian Floor Show" in the midst of the night to break the mood, to reestablish balance and control.

A strong note of authority is essential. Fifty people a night are needed on the team to staff the Cabaret. Some must be strong adults. Liquor poses problems. The two adults on the door we call the "Watcher" and the "Sniffer." One excludes those who do not reach our standards of dress, the other tries to detect the alcoholic breath. No pass-out checks are allowed, to block young people from going out to nearby hotels during the night. Without the strongest control, with six hundred teenagers, trouble is ahead.

What are the fruits of Teenage Cabaret? They are many. The Holy Spirit bears his own witness through the messages given. One night a boy spoke to me. I knew him, he had recently been released from a boy's reformatory for car stealing. "I don't know what's come over me," he said. "The other night I was going to 'pinch' a car. It was a 'cinch.' Even the key was there. I was just getting in when I remembered something you said at Cabaret. I walked away. I don't know what's happened to me."

We have seen many teenage conversions over the years

72

from those who have come on from Cabaret to Sunday worship. The flow from Cabaret into the church is only a trickle, but, apart from all else that happens, it justifies all the effort. Above all we find when in any kind of trouble youth turns to us, whom they know, for help. Then is the hour of opportunity for witness.

Building on experience and links through Teenage Cabaret we hold special teenage services. For these the foundation is the same interest in fast beat music, the guitar, and the band and direct Christian testimony.

As part of the annual Easter Mission to Sydney we conduct, we have a great teenage night—the Easter Parade—in the city's largest auditorium, the Sydney Town Hall. Three thousand teenagers throng the building, most of them beyond the normal ministries of the church.

As the lights dim in the Town Hall, there is a youth choir, a band, and the night's master of ceremonies on the stage. In smooth, fast tempo the program begins. There are some of the teenage "stars" present. They sing, some secular songs but mostly songs with something of a religious content.

Audience participation is important. How teenagers like to clap and sway in rhythm to "He's Got the Whole World in His Hands" or "When the Saints Go Marching In." It is rather raucous, but perhaps it can be interpreted as making a "joyful noise unto the Lord." It is certainly noisy.

Throughout the night testimonies are given. Brian Booth, the Australian cricketer, tells of his Christian faith. He is followed by Ian Moutray, an international footballer, and Bruce Menzies, an Australian television personality. The teenagers listen intently. They are impressed that people they admire are practicing Christians.

As the main address comes near there is a slight change of mood. The songs sung by the artists and the choir become quieter, aimed at quietening the audience. Then comes the message. An amazing silence settles over the auditorium, as the gospel wins its way.

The climax is an open evangelistic appeal. As the band leads the singing of "Just a Closer Walk with Thee," an invitation is given to come forward, by so doing making a first commitment to Jesus Christ. Slowly the response begins, and soon a stream of teenagers are taken by prepared youth counselors who try to tell how to enter the kingdom of God.

At last all is over. Young Sydney streams out into the soft Australian autumn night. In our hearts there is a deep thankfulness. We know that all the struggle and effort of youth programs and Teenage Cabaret are all worth while. We have seen Christ at work amid the lost and lonely teenagers of today's world.

The Servant Church in Action

Two great incidents took place in the Last Supper Room in Jerusalem on the night before Jesus was crucified. In the first, Jesus took bread and wine, symbols of his coming death, and handed them to his disciples. By this act he instituted the most solemn and unique ceremony of the Christian church. Quietly his disciples heard him say: "Do this in remembrance of me" (Luke 22:19).

In the second incident, Jesus took a towel and a basin and in the role of a servant washed the travel-stained feet of his men. This, too, he commanded should forever be repeated by His followers: "You also ought to wash one another's feet. . . . you also should do as I have done to you" (John 13:14-15).

So, using the word loosely, Jesus gave two sacraments to his Church: bread and wine and a towel and a basin. By word and example Jesus called his church to be the servant church, humbly meeting the needs of men.

The church has listened and obeyed the words of Jesus relating to bread and wine far more than his summons to service. What God has joined together, man has put asunder. Some Christians concentrate endlessly on Holy Communion. The church has almost overemphasized bread and wine at the expense of the towel and basin.

On the other hand, some Christians have tried to use the towel and basin of service without receiving the grace which comes through Holy Communion. The sin of the church has been to neglect service; the sin of the world is neglect of Communion. Jesus, in the amazing balance of his life, kept both in balance together.

How often the church has forgotten that it exists to serve, and even when it has remembered, its servantship has been corrupted by lordship. Over the years in societies where the Christian faith is the accepted faith of the people, privilege has been accorded the church. Privilege accepted soon becomes privilege expected. The servant, presently, demands to be served.

There is so much in the modern church which gives a false image of the gospel to the world. What right has a follower of Jesus to be called a "prince of the church"—a prince! How has it come about that a bishop is called "lord?" Humility has given place to grandeur in the mansions and palaces in which church leaders sometimes live.

Vividly I remember one picture at the Third Assembly of the World Council of Churches at New Delhi. It was of a confessional leader of one of the participating churches arriving in his rather gaudy attire, stepping from a chauffeur-driven Rolls Royce through some Indian beggars who had gathered. If ever the lordly rather than the servant church was apparent it was, for me at least, at that moment.

A similar vignette comes from New Guinea. At an all-day conference hundreds of Papuan catechists and ministers and a few white missionaries poured out of the large thatched-roof church following the morning session. At once I was taken with the white missionaries to a table spread with bountiful food in the cool beneath the trees. The Papuan ministers squatted under nearby trees. Again I was conscious that even amid the magnificent service of the missionary church, master-servant and privileged concepts can creep in almost unnoticed.

Perhaps all of us who stand within the life of the church need to hear the reminder Bruce Kendrick gives in *The New Humanity*, that Jesus said: "As my Father sent me, even so send I you." Then he adds: "He had been sent to identify Himself unreservedly with men, to share their sorrows, their griefs, their sufferings; to penetrate into the depths of their lives, to be wounded, to bleed and to die. That was how the Father sent Him. And now send I you."

What should be the relationship between church and state? There are Christians who look upon the state as existing to serve, obey the church. There are others who would separate church and state, but this usually means asking the state at least to protect, to make easy the work of the church. The truth is the church exists to serve the state. It is when the church accepts its role of service within the community that its noblest work is done.

There is developing in Australia a fruitful new relationship between church and state. It is one in which

77

both church and state accept the servantship of the church.

It took clearest expression in this way. The federal government became convinced it must set out in a new way to care for the aged and especially the sick and frail, aged poor. The prime minister looked to the churches to help. He said: "It is not the task of the government to establish a department of Christian charity." So by offering heavy subsidies, the government decided to provide the money if the church would accept the responsibility and provide the dedicated people who would serve the needs of the people.

Today the government of Australia provides a two pounds to one subsidy to churches and approved community organizations for the establishment of homes for the aged. In addition, under certain conditions, continuing assistance in maintenance of the homes is available.

As a result scores of homes and hospitals for the aged have been built across Australia. Through them the churches have found a role of service in cooperation with the state which fulfills their ministry. With Christian compassion the needs of the helpless are being met. It is having its place in the mission of the church, winning a hearing for the gospel which inspires such service.

The importance of the serving church was recognized by the founding in 1884 in Sydney of the first Central Methodist Mission. With prophetic vision the Reverend W. G. Taylor in that year saw that the spoken word and the service of the people should be expressed together. As a result of the leadership then given in every major Australian city, the central church of Methodism bears the name Central Methodist Mission and is committed to a particular policy.

The essence of the policy is that Christian service agencies such as children's homes, hospitals, and homes for the aged are initiated and maintained by the congregation of the city church. This means that these agencies, rather than directed by boards of the synods or conferences of the denomination, are the responsibility of a living congregation of worshiping Christians. And this, I believe, is an important concept, for it binds together in fact and in the public mind an evangelical witness and the meeting of human need in the community.

Today the Central Methodist Mission in Sydney controls fourteen homes, hospitals, and hostels. It cares for children through three children's homes, one of which is a short-term emergency refuge for children in sudden need. It has a hostel for Australian and overseas students. An Evangelists' Institute, where young men and women receive training for Christian witness and service, performs a vital task. It operates a Night Refuge for homeless men. It has initiated Australia's only Christian psychiatric hospital. Care for the aged is expressed through four residential homes for senior citizens. It directs a fine long-term or terminal hospital.

The Mission today has within its care 730 people every day and night of the year. This necessitates a full-time staff of 260 people and an annual budget of $1,200,000. The important fact is that the same ministers, the same Board of Management, are responsible for the evangelistic ministry of a great city church and a vast service program. I dare to claim that the strength of the Sydney Central

Methodist Mission over all these years is explained by the fact that it has had in its hands both bread and wine and a towel and basin.

The most important social-religious idea yet developed by the Central Methodist Mission in Sydney is called Life Line. After four years of planning it began operation in March, 1963. Since that time it has grown amazingly, offering a vital service in a mass society. It is the servant church in action.

Life Line was born in the discovery of the ocean of need which seethes beneath the life of a great city. Over the years we had become oppressed by the number of people who, seemingly not knowing where to turn in an hour of need, came to us. Often, we realized, the first point of contact was a telephone call.

Significant changes have overtaken a city of 2,500,000 people like Sydney. Half the population never goes to church, so all links with the neighborhood minister have been lost. People are now embarrassed to enter a minister's residence or a church.

Once the family physician fulfilled an important role in a community as the confidant of many. Today, with panels of doctors replacing the older more personal medical practice, intimacy and confidence have to a large degree declined.

So a vacuum has appeared. Where do people turn? The police, the psychiatrist, a government officer are all, for various reasons, avoided.

I remember a woman calling in the middle of the night. She apologized for waking me. She was desperate with anxiety over family problems. She had to talk to somebody. For half an hour she poured out her troubles. I asked her why she had called me. She gave an answer which revealed a lot. "You do not know me, you live far from my suburb. And anyway, you cannot see the tears running down my cheeks."

Many experiences of this kind lay behind the first entry I find in my diary in August, 1958. "There has been taking shape in my mind over many weeks the idea of an organization to meet human need called 'The Mantle of Christ.'"

Then came the clue which allowed all to fall into place. That clue was the telephone. Why not exploit the ubiquitous telephone. There could run a thin line of relationship from hundreds of thousands of telephones throughout the metropolis to a central point of residence where need could be met.

There stands today in the heart of Sydney the Life Line Center. Built at a cost of $120,000, it says to the whole city: Help is as close as the telephone. With its telephone number listed in the emergency page of the telephone directory with fire brigades and ambulances, it has become an essential service. Many wonder how Sydney lived without it.

The Life Line telephones are staffed twenty-four hours a day by mature Christian volunteers who have passed through a training course and, after being interviewed, are accredited for the task.

There are four shifts each day: 8 A.M. to 12:30 P.M.; 12:30 P.M. to 5:30 P.M.; 5:30 P.M. to 10 P.M.; 10 P.M. to 8 A.M. the next morning. In other words, the Life Line phones are never unattended, giving to the city an image of the Bible message that "God never sleeps."

81

When the telephone rings a voice says: "This is the Life Line Center, can I help you?" As the caller talks, notes are made from which a report sheet is later filled. Where some follow-up is required—as it is in fifty per cent of the cases—the caller is asked to call back the next day after 11: 30 A.M., by which time an interview will be arranged with an appropriate counselor.

Each morning an Assignment Committee made up of senior staff members of the Center consider all reports. Appointments are made with ministers, social workers, psychiatrists, marriage guidance counselors, youth advisors. So the follow-through begins. Life Line remembers that the good Samaritan in Christ's parable did not only offer first aid, he stayed with the stricken man until again, from the inn to which he was taken, he could proceed on his way.

Life Line tries to offer answers in depth to all who turn for help. The telephone counselors are the contact people. Behind them are the thirteen full-time staff members who have become necessary to handle the volume of work which has developed. There are a hundred professional people—doctors, psychiatrists, lawyers, businessmen—who in an honorary capacity take up to three cases at a time. Beyond all this assistance stand the fourteen homes and hospitals of the Central Methodist Mission and other agencies in the city to which, where it is wise, people may be directed.

An important feature of Life Line is the "Caring Division." It is composed of another group of volunteers who are willing to offer friendship to people needing rehabilitation for up to a period of three months. It is the task of members of the Caring Division to telephone or visit or write to those allotted to them and to report as to further needs or problems which may develop.

Group therapy is also attempted. Two "New Life" groups meet, in which alcoholics and compulsive gamblers, on the one hand, and people in psychiatric need meet. Group guidance is also offered to the many unmarried mothers-to-be who turn to Life Line.

Life Line has an emergency division, for the Center offers a suicide prevention service to Sydney. The Center is equipped with three radio-controlled cars. A "Trouble Team" of two people is always on call and is capable of rushing into any situation across the city which may demand urgent action.

At the heart of all that is done through the Life Line Center is the Life Line Movement. It is the "discipleship in depth" program of the Central Methodist Mission. All who serve through the Center must first join the Movement, for only through a disciplined laity can the work be maintained.

Membership in the Life Line Movement is open to all who are members of the Christian church and who are willing to accept the discipline of the movement. Applicants are obliged to attend a prescribed course of lectures and are interviewed by the movement's executive before being accepted. The fivefold pledge which all must take has as its first requirement: "I accept Jesus Christ as my Savior and Lord." In other words, only convinced and practicing Christians may belong to the movement.

Lay Christians have shown an amazing enthusiasm for the service and witness opened to them through the movement. Most come from the congregation of the Central Methodist Mission, but increasingly people are applying from other Methodist churches and other denominations. We are glimpsing a little of what could happen when the "sleeping giant" of the church, the laity, awakens.

As the opening day for Life Line came near, we became anxious. We had plunged $120,000 on the assumption that there was a tremendous area of unmet need in a mass society and that people would turn to such a center. What was to happen?

Worry was wasted. The telephones were opened at 5:30 P.M. on March 16, 1963, and they have scarcely stopped ringing since. During the second year, 1964, there were 10,033 people who as first contacts turned to Life Line. They covered the whole range of human need from simple loneliness to suicidal despair.

A breakdown of the reports dealt with by the Center shows the following picture:

714	Marriage Guidance
560	Alcoholics
240	Unmarried Mothers
75	Compulsive Gamblers
24	Drug addicts

During this year, suicidal calls totaled 312, or 26 each month.

Incidents speak louder than statistics. Two nights following a fourteen-year-old boy called near midnight, lonely and frightened because his parents were out, just wanting to talk to someone.

A young man, learning that week he was stricken with

84

cancer with six months to live, wanted to discuss the meaning of life and death.

A suspected murderer, cornered by the police in an outer suburb house, rang Life Line as the police cordon closed in. "Can you help me?" was his plea.

A stranger asked a passer-by where he could get a bus to Watson's Bay. Noticing the emotional condition of the enquirer, and knowing that Watson's Bay was the site of Australia's most notorious suicides' jumping-off place called "the Gap," that passer-by called Life Line. By quick action Life Line was able to intercept a young school-teacher, jilted by his fiancée, and draw him back from the edge of the precipice.

Why do people call Life Line? I am convinced the one who prompts many a person in the hour of need to reach for a telephone is the Holy Spirit. In too many cases there is a mystery about the rings which come; it can only be explained in theological terms.

The Holy Spirit, as promised by Jesus, has an interior access into human consciousness. He cannot coerce human personality, but he can suggest, guide. Where a man or woman has at some time heard of Life Line, he can bring a remembrance of it to mind at the moment of need.

Let me illustrate. Late one night the Life Line phone rang. It was a man at a phone booth at the end of the Sydney Harbor Bridge, threatening to throw himself to death. Quickly the "Trouble Team" was despatched. The man, hopelessly in debt from gambling, afraid to tell his wife, saw but one way out. He was actually climbing the bridge railing when the thought came: Isn't there a place called Life Line? Walking to the telephone booth he tried to call but could not find the number. Returning, he again began climbing, and again felt an inner pressure to try Life Line. This time he succeeded and the rescue, therapy, caring program of Life Line swung into action and a life was not only saved but, over months of help, rehabilitated.

Life Line is spreading in a remarkable way. After two years, centers were opened in the Australian cities of Brisbane, Adelaide, Broken Hill, in Christchurch, New Zealand, in Cape Town, South Africa. From all over the world, interest has flowed.

Through it—the servant church in action—I can see a new strategy in a mass society. The neighborhood church will remain the basic unit in the strategy of Jesus. But I can see superimposed upon it a central agency like Life Line to which people, alienated from the church, may more readily turn. Then, back to the neighborhood church, when agreement to do so is gained, can the individual be directed. There the local minister, fellowship groups, worship experience may be found.

Recently I visited the Australian town of Bathurst, 130 miles from Sydney, and was introduced to a woman who sat opposite me at a church supper. I remember her story. Months before she had called Life Line, claiming she had a double-barreled shotgun between her knees and was going to end her life. The telephone counselor reasoned with her for thirty-five minutes, then the phone went silent.

Acting quickly, the counselor telephoned the Bathurst Methodist minister. He in turn called a Christian couple at a nearby farm. They hurried to their neighbor's home and found the woman, distraught, still clutching the gun. They managed to get it from her, just as the minister arrived. With her consent she was taken for psychiatric care to a hospital. The local church continued its pastoral care. As I looked at that woman, I could only think of the words of the New Testament concerning the deranged man in the country of the *Gerasenes*. "They found the man . . . sitting at the feet of Jesus, clothed and in his right mind" (Luke 8:35).

Life Line is Christian. No attempt is made to force religion on anyone who calls. However, it is our conviction that we cannot answer human need—even the most simple case of social distress—without seeing every life in the context of the spiritual.

Therefore, while every technical skill is pressed into service, it is people who are Christian whom we want at the telephones, in our specialized services, in the Caring Division. And while the purpose of Life Line is to meet need, with no strings attached, with no ulterior motive, we realize that we cannot fully meet that need without pointing those who come to Christ the Savior and Healer of men. Into the fellowship of the church, many a lonely life would best find its way. We know that worship can be the best therapy of all.

In Life Line we have seen the servant church in action. Through it the laity has discovered a new ministry. By it we are seeing the mission of Christ carried out into the world.

The Church that only worships dies. Bread and wine, towel and basin must all be in the hands of the followers of Jesus. There is no other way to go on mission. As H. Berkof of Holland once said at a World Council of Churches meeting: "A preaching church without a life of works of love and mercy has no winning power. Witness without service is empty. Service without witness is dumb."

The Atomic Power of the Laity

One day in 1939 two German scientists succeeded in splitting the uranium atom. At once the way was open for the release of undreamed of power for human use. By isolating matter to its small particle, the atom, and then tapping the vast energy stored within it, the whole human scene has been transformed.

There is a small unit within the Christian church. It is the life and witness of every layman and laywoman who accepts membership in the church. Within each one are untapped resources, powers which, if released, could transform the church and the world.

How shall the atomic power of the laity be let loose? On the answer to this question depends the very future of the influence of the Christian church in today's world. Only through the total ministry of the church—of ordained ministers and the laity working together in witness

—shall the gospel penetrate into the lives of people and the structures of society.

The doctrine of the "priesthood of all believers" was one of the great rediscoveries of the Protestant Reformation. Unfortunately, just as John Wesley's emphasis on holiness or Christian perfection was never developed by the Methodists, so the doctrine of the "priesthood of all believers" has remained static since the Reformation. For some reason, the church simply has not followed the insight of Martin Luther. We have even forgotten that it was Luther who gave to the world the concept of "vocational guidance." There has been an almost complete failure in theological or in practical terms to spell out the meaning of the ministry of the laity.

The Christian layman today has not learned to live as a layman out in the world. Some laymen hide their Christian allegiance. Reticent about mentioning or discussing religious questions, they make little or no witness to people with whom they work. Others keep the two segments of their lives, Christian faith and daily involvement in the world, separate. There is no recognition of the fact that to be a Christian doctor or a Christian carpenter is very different from a doctor and a Christian or a Christian and a carpenter.

There is a type of layman who is as "clericalized" as a minister. This was shown to me recently when I sought the help of a professional man in bringing people within his own profession, who had no Christian allegiance, to a dinner. There was not one of this type, he confessed, with whom he had any links. He did not attend any professional society; he spent no time with any other than a few known Christians. He gave all his time to church meetings. He thought like a minister, lived like a minister, acted like a minister. Though in the world, he was not of it in any real sense. He might as well have been ordained!

It was at the Third Assembly of the World Council of Churches where many Christian leaders from around the world began to see a new role for the laity. This assembly gathered up and with power expressed a decade of prophetic thinking and writing concerning the mission of the Christian out in the world.

Miss E. M. Batten of England likened the Christian laymen to paratroopers. In developing the metaphor, she said: "Local churches must be seen as supply depots rather than 'arks of safety.' The Church will be a place for the parachutists to call in for the Apostles' teaching, that is for briefing for their work in the world; for fellowship in order to encourage one another for the next bit of active service; for the breaking of bread—the sacraments —through which they will be cleaned-up and refitted for their next spell of duty; for the prayers in which they will lay before God their concerns and receive new light to go out for their witness—that is the faithful carrying out of their responsibilities as they respond to the demands made upon them in the structures of the world."

There can be no releasing of the atomic power of the laity in the world without a training program for the laity within the life of the church. In the final report of the New Delhi Assembly of the World Council of Churches appears this sentence: "Every church spends great sums of money on training ministers, nothing on training laymen and women to do God's work out in a secular world where ninety-nine per cent of Christians must be."

Training must be of two elements. One is the teaching of the gospel, of biblical and theological truth. The other is to probe in Christian terms into the structures of the world. Without a knowledge of Christian doctrine a layman is unable to give a good account of the faith which is in him. Without the ability to relate his gospel relevantly to society, he is likely to be no different in mental attitude from those about him who own to no Christian belief or allegiance.

A sobering survey was taken in an American city. The mental attitude of people on a number of vital current national and international issues was sought. One group was composed of people who regularly worshiped and were therefore exposed to the thinking of the pulpit and the church. The other was of people who had no regular encounter with the church. An analysis showed that the views of both groups were the same. In other words, the Christians might just as well have not gone regularly to church. Christian truth had no observable effect on their minds.

The lay training policy of the Sydney Central Methodist Mission is expressed through what is called College for Christians. There come together every Tuesday night a company of up to two hundred people for a serious adult Christian education program.

College for Christians begins at 6:30 P.M. with a lecture on Christian doctrine on biblical knowledge. The lecture is followed by the membership being broken up into ten or twelve discussion groups. Care is taken to fashion groups of varying types of people. There is a circle largely made up of new Christians. Under another leader is an "advanced" class where the level of discussion is much higher. There are also two youth classes.

Each group, in directed discussion, considers five questions written beneath the mimeographed synopsis of the lecture which has been handed to them. On one of the questions a report, in one sentence, is to be made of the conclusions of the group. At the end of the discussion session all reassemble to hear the report on the same chosen question from each group. Some of the answers demand omnibus sentences, but the interest is keen to compare answer with answer.

At 8 P.M. a series of lectures is available on particular subjects which concern the laity in service within the church and witness out in the world.

It is amazing how limited are the tasks offered to laymen and women in the average church. I heard, for example, an explosive criticism of the church by an able, university trained woman who offered assistance to her local church and was asked to bake a cake for the coming church fete! No wonder some of the finest men and women turn from the church to fashion substitute interest and service organizations within the wider community.

What a commentary on the church—the church which was given by Christ a towel and a basin—that so-called "service clubs" are part of every town and suburb. Rotary, Lions, Kiwanis clubs often achieve what should be the task of the servant church.

In recent years there has been much theoretic talk of the need for mobilizing the laity for service and witness.

So much is theoretic; it breaks down at the point of "how"? How does the church utilize the vast manpower resources of the laity?

The life and witness of our church in Sydney has been transformed since we established the Life Line Movement as a "discipleship in depth" program among our people.

The Life Line Movement is not primarily an organization but a spiritual commitment to Christ and his church. Its purpose is fourfold: to seek personal holiness of life, growth in Christian knowledge, dedication to service, and witness in society.

Membership is open to all who are members of the Christian church and who are willing to accept the discipline of the movement. Members are required to accept the following pledge:

I accept Jesus Christ as my Savior and Lord.

I seek by personal piety, and corporate prayer, to grow in holiness and to be a channel of God's grace.

I seek to grow in Christian knowledge through Bible study, weekly attendance at Sunday worship, and such training courses as may be available.

I accept, after consultation, the place and service to which I may be appointed in the Life Line Movement and the church.

We have seen faith come alive as members have found the joy of service. Especially direct service and witness in the mission of the church have brought enthusiasm. Too often we ask the laity to go on mission by proxy—through the gift of money and support for others who proclaim the gospel—rather than fashioning situations in which they may do it themselves. Even simple and humble tasks within the life of the church have taken on a new purpose when interpreted as being part of the mission of Christ, ever remembering that the servant is no greater than his master who washed the disciples' feet.

The chief service and witness of the laity must be given not within the church, but out in the world. It is within the secular structures of society that the decisions are made which determine the quality of society and so deeply affect the lives of millions.

Elton Trueblood in *The Company of the Committed* points out that when Christ sought to communicate to his disciples the nature of his cause he used metaphors of penetration. His followers are called upon to be salt, light, leaven. The purpose of salt is to penetrate meat and preserve it. The function of light is to banish the darkness by penetrating it. Leaven must enter the dough and work as a ferment right through it if the bread is to rise.

It is the laity, not the ministry, to whom the privilege of penetration into the world is given. Yet how often the Christian fails to see this task.

"What you need is a deaconess," a professional social worker said to me recently in refusing a task within a Christian organization. Though claiming to be a committed Christian, she kept her professional thinking and Christian belief in two compartments. She could not see that the Christian faith has little meaning if it does not become the framework of reference in which work is carried on within the various segments of society.

There is a great story in Acts of how a man within the structures of society bore witness to justice and truth and was able to turn the tide. It is the story of what happened when Peter and the Apostles were dragged before the Sanhedrin in Jerusalem.

Amid the bigotry and the hatred, as injustice was ready to be done, Gamaliel arose. "Men of Israel," he said, "take care what you do with these men. . . . if this plan or this undertaking is of men, it will fail; but if it is of God, you will not be able to overthrow them. You might even be found opposing God" (Acts 5: 35-39).

"They took his advice . . . and let them go." Gamaliel turned the tide by making his witness to the truth within the structures of society. As a layman, out in the world, he stood for God.

The Mass Communication
of a Personal Gospel

The gospel of Jesus is personal through and through. The love of God is a general love for all mankind, but its very essence is that it is particular and individual. Christ was constantly halted by some case of personal need. He said, beautifully, that there is joy in heaven when a sinner repents, when someone who is lost is found.

Mass meetings and mass media treat people in the mass. Large gatherings submerge people, so it seems, in an ocean of conformity. The gospel has to be shouted across distances, with mechanical amplification widening the gulf between speaker and audience. The personal touch appears to be lost. Similarly, numbers seem all that matter in television and radio where rating scales are the Bible of program designers and network executives. Individuals who are different, minority groups, are of little importance in mass communication. Average interests and emotions, the secret of how to appeal to millions dominate planning. To have people thinking together, laughing together, feeling together is the fundamental aim and, where it succeeds, the result of mass media.

How can a personal gospel be communicated in a mass way? God honors a person by speaking directly to him, by listening as he replies. Christ deals supremely with the individual needs of individual people. To offer humanity the gospel in the mass seems to be a contradiction in terms and purpose.

When the Holy Spirit takes charge there can be mass communication and personal receiving. This is the meaning of Pentecost. On the day of Pentecost in Jerusalem, there was a company of people together—a mass meeting —and the Spirit fell upon them. But it was a personal receiving. "There appeared to them tongues as of fire, distributed and resting on each of them" (Acts 2:3).

Peter then went out and preached to a great company of people. It must have been a mass meeting of large dimensions, for about three thousand were that day added to the infant church. The story says: "Each one heard them speaking in his own language" (Acts 2:6).

A commentary on the happenings on the day of Pentecost was given in the Mission to Fiji. We had deep concern over the language problem, for we knew many Fijians could not readily understand or speak English. At the opening meeting we decided to use an interpreter. Seven thousand people thronged Albert Park in Suva for the opening meeting.

Next day there was a stream of callers and numbers of phone calls to Methodist headquarters all protesting against the use of an interpreter. We understood, the Fijians said. So we abandoned offering a translation. Night by night the thousands came, and during that two-week mission, 2,439 people personally responded to the call to commit their lives to Jesus Christ.

Here was the use of the mass meeting. It proved that personal acceptance of the gospel came through mass communication. The barrier of language somehow was defeated. After that mission in Fiji, I read the story of Acts with new understanding: "Each one heard them speaking in his own language."

Mass evangelism is one method of evangelism, and a very effective instrument in mission. God does speak to individuals within the crowd. The very largeness and enthusiasm of big meetings kindle faith and hope, especially among faithful Christians who spend their days serving small churches. In today's society, without large-scale gatherings, it is difficult to gain a place in the press for the proclamation of a Christian message.

During the fifties there were two great Christian ventures in Australia which used mass evangelism: the Methodist Mission to the Nation and the Billy Graham Crusade to Australia. One result of these efforts was a considerable lift in the intake of candidates for the ministry. Apparently God spoke to many young men as they assembled amid the crowds, and spoke with such strength that the course of their life was deflected. As a result the chronic manpower shortage of the Australian ministry was eased. It is significant that now, as the impact of these two evangelistic thrusts recedes into the past, the number of candidates for the ministry is falling.

I believe profoundly in mass evangelism. Sometimes it seems the biting criticisms by certain churchmen of those who have the abilities to gather and address large meetings seem to reflect, not objective analysis of the facts, but their own inability to draw people together. The proclaiming by the preacher of the gospel of Jesus to crowds is one way by which the kingdom spreads.

There is only one way quickly to reach mass man in a mass society; it is by mass media. Personal evangelism, the house church, the coffee shop, the neighborhood church, all have their place. All are small and slow. All need the assistance which the presentation of the gospel can supply when broadcast by mass media.

The church has never really learned to live amid mass media. Fearful of it, slow to conquer the new techniques involved, unable to command the finance necessary for adequate use of it, the greatest opportunity to proclaim the gospel in all history has been largely missed.

"Using mass media is like boring for oil," one of Australia's leading advertising executives said recently to me. "An oil company, spending a large sum of money, reaches a certain depth. It stops, perhaps running out of money. Had it continued another five hundred feet, it would have struck oil. By stopping short it not only failed to get oil, it lost all it cost to go as far as it did.

"The church often wastes money in trying to use mass media. It just will not persist far enough or long enough to get results. Much of what is spent is lost, for the impact is too infrequent or too slight to register."

There is a sense of restraint by many in the Christian use of mass media. It is bound up with the question of how far a gospel which ever respects human personality can go. After all, the Christian serves a God who is ready to halt at the threshold of every life, refusing to force entrance. One of the noblest sentences in the Bible is in the Book of Revelation: "Behold, I stand at the door and knock; if any one hears my voice and opens the door, I will come in to him and eat with him and he with me" (Rev. 3:20).

There is an issue here of integrity for the church. Perhaps more effective results could be obtained by more skilful use, shall we say, of television. Perhaps a saturation campaign could be undertaken which would almost oblige all to hear and see a Christian campaign. But should it be done? There is only one answer. The church can never forget the principle once enunciated by Herbert Farmer in his book *The Servant of the Word:* "The preacher must deeply reverence in his hearer what has been called the sacred right of rejection, even in the midst of his passionate desire for acceptance."

There is a long-range result from mass witness which the Christian church is justified in seeking. It is that the level of understanding and acceptance by people of the Christian faith can be raised until it becomes possible for them to move toward full commitment to Christ.

Let me explain what I mean. The church knows what it is to experience a mass movement into the Christian faith. It has happened, especially in Indian missionary work where, after years of seemingly fruitless witness, whole villages seek baptism.

Why? How does it happen? Steadily over the years

there has grown an awareness of Christian truth. Prejudices have been broken down, a knowledge of Christian doctrine has developed. At last some event, some movement of the Spirit's coming, causes some village leader or some family to embrace Christianity. Scores, hundreds may follow. It is not as shallow a happening as it on the surface appears. It is the fruit of faithful witness by word of mouth and quality of life for long, seemingly disappointing years.

The rightful use of mass media over a lengthy period of time could in a modern society have a similar result. At present it is working in reverse, for television, radio, and the printed page are canceling out so many of the impressions made within the life of the church. By telling faithfully and well the Christian story through mass media, the day could come when there could be a moving by whole sections of the community toward a personal acceptance of God in Christ. In that day we would see with new insight that there can be the mass communication of a personal gospel.

It is amazing the way the major churches in countries like America and Australia have allowed fringe Christian groups to dominate radio. Smaller Christian groups with less institutional religion to support, have discovered the power of radio even in a television age.

For years I have conducted concurrently radio and television programs. This experience has proved the value of radio. In some ways it seems to have a greater spiritual impact than television. Perhaps it is because the lack of visual aids brings closer concentration to the voice and message, perhaps there is an intimacy and directness in radio speech which makes for deeper impact, but whatever it is, radio possesses tremendous power to reach the individual lives of people.

There is another reason. Perhaps radio, by its very nature encourages, emphasizes direct witness to Christ. In other words proclamation, preaching is called forth by the nature of radio.

The church has often been sidetracked by television, sidetracked into secondary forms of witness. Drama, panel discussions, documentaries have been the chosen vehicle of so much religious television. No one would depreciate their use or their impact, but often they have been used to the neglect of preaching.

Television is made for preaching. By mastering television techniques, but then to place directly before the people the story of the mighty acts of God, is to release a larger measure of the power of Christian truth than in any other way.

The longest running Christian television program in Australia is one called "I Challenge the Minister," discontinued only recently after seven years of broadcast.

The format of "I Challenge the Minister" is a simple one. An audience is gathered either in a studio or out on location. As the cameras begin to whir, I give a two- or three-minute introduction aimed at provoking questions. Then it is a case of over to the audience. Questions are invited and an off-the-cuff answer is attempted. The give and take of questions and answers continues for twenty-five minutes. As many as twelve or fifteen questions are possible in the time. At the close there is again a brief summing-up, the issuing of a challenge.

At no time have I ever known the terms of any question asked. Part of the appeal of the session is its "quiz" element. There is uncertainty as to whether an answer will be given. Brief answers are attempted, the average being of one minute duration.

The fact that there is camera variety aids the session. The camera focuses on the questioner as the answer is spoken into a trailing microphone. Audience reactions are telecast as the cameras frequently rove over the faces of the people present.

Undoubtedly the most effective telecasts have come from out-of-doors. Sessions have been held on wharves, in railroad workshops, at factories, schools, and universities. Each summer "I Challenge the Minister" has been telecast on a Sunday afternoon from the center of one of Sydney's beaches with its teeming sun and surf bathers.

Questions on any subject are accepted. With Christ as the Lord of all life, no question is barred. Broadly speaking, they fall into three categories. There are doctrinal and biblical questions, personal problems appear, and social, national, and international issues are raised.

Naturally the topical determines many a question. Following a fatal shark tragedy on one of our beaches came the question: "Why does God make sharks?" In factories and workshops, questions on peace and war come more frequently than any other, showing the real puzzlement of the working classes about the failure of the church to grapple with international affairs.

The chief requirement of this kind of program is frankness. No audience reacts adversely when the honest reply is given: "I don't know." Confidence is lost if the impression is received that one is not honest in the answer given or that the speaker is playing safe on some current issue.

Controversy is always near. The speaker, of course, cannot control the subjects chosen as in a prepared address or sermon. Hence the seven years of witness have been marked by several sharp controversies which have broken into the press. Only gain has come from such occurrences, as public interest has been further stimulated.

As with all use of mass media, results are hard to tabulate. It is clear that according to the rating scales "I Challenge the Minister" has consistently won larger viewing audiences than any other Australian religious program. Certainly many a personal contact has been established, many a pastoral opportunity has developed, many a person has appeared at worship because of the session.

Mass media for mission has many limitations. It turns people into spectators rather than participants. It offers no ongoing fellowship which is so much a part of the ministry of the church. It allows no follow-through unless further links are established.

Mass media is primarily a contact method. By it people are reached who today will not enter a church building. It often wins a bridgehead in some mind previously estranged and prejudiced against the Christian position.

Follow-up is all-important. Somehow mass communication must become individual and personal if it is fully to take its place in the mission of Jesus.

There is working as an ordained minister in Australian Methodism today a young man whose life illustrates how mass media can be used to the utmost by the Spirit of God. From Germany he came as a migrant. Settling as a farm assistant in Western Australia he listened frequently to radio in an effort to improve his English. He discovered a weekly Australian Christian program, "Drama with a Challenge," which was then heard across the nation.

As a former Hitler Youth, he had no knowledge of the Christian faith. Intrigued by its presentation of Christian truth he asked his employer about it. His employer, a Methodist layman, introduced him to worship, and to a youth discussion group. Months later a mass mission was held in the Perth City Hall. One night carloads of people drove the one hundred miles from this country area to share in the meetings. The young German was among them. At the close of the meeting an open evangelistic appeal was issued, and this man came forward, committing his life to Jesus Christ. Still later, he heard the call to enter the Christian ministry. Accepted for training, he moved toward ordination. Today he effectively serves his church in the Australian ministry.

Here is an example of how mass media may be used by the Holy Spirit. Of itself, radio could have done little. It was the vital initial point of relationship without which nothing else may have followed. Yet the total ministry of the church had to be added: lay witness, the fellowship of the neighborhood church, a teaching witness, mass evangelism, training for service. It is in this kind of context mass media takes a rightful and vital place.

The mission of Jesus in today's world must include the mass communication of a personal gospel.

The world today is a pre-Christian world. In the past the Christian faith has entered powerfully into many lives and has penetrated far into some areas of western society. But the world has never been Christian, for in no society have Christians been more than a minority. Even where personal piety has been strong there has been a failure to influence deeply the secular structures of society.

Talk of today being a "post-Christian society" seems to me to be false. When was the world Christian, from which level is it now supposed to have retreated? It was certainly not Christian in the Middle Ages, when life was crude, brutish, and short. Nor was it Christian in the eighteenth and nineteenth centuries with slavery, colonialism, and industrial exploitation of the working classes. The first half of the twentieth century does not deserve the title, for war upon war with the increasing descent to barbarism disqualifies it.

108

Hence the Christian mission must be advanced in a pre-Christian world, and this must include the proclamation of the prophet in society. There is no doubt that countless people are today beyond the ministry of the church because of the past failure of the church to be truly prophetic in critical hours of history. Because of the silence, the conservatism of the church at the beginning of the Industrial Revolution and as the exploitation of men, women, and children deepened, industrial man turned his back on the Christian faith, never as yet to be regained.

John MacMurray, in *It's My Belief*, is virtually spokesman for millions who reject the church because of war. "I came out of the First World War convinced that there must be something radically wrong with a civilisation which issued in such a tragedy. Since it was confessedly a Christian tradition, the doubt for many fastened upon its Christianity. I felt the strain in my own life. From that time I have not found it possible to identify myself with any Church. The doubt had gone too deep."

I wish I could be sure past mistakes are not being repeated. The servant church which becomes merely an ambulance church, caring for the injured found along the highways of our society, yet doing nothing about the forces which produce the injury, is only half a church.

The chaplaincy church which sends its representatives into industry or the armed forces to serve the men who are there, but never question the structure of capitalism or the nature of war, will forfeit basic respect. The counseling church which pours its man-hours into marriage guidance and neurotic casework and is silent on the nature of a society which produces breakdowns is an escapist church.

The church carries peculiar responsibilities because of the freedom it enjoys. After all it is the freest institution in society. Financial support is widely based. It is largely free from the fear of economic penalties which affect many another institution dependent on financial support from big business or government. A Christian minister rarely faces the threat of dismissal for what he says. He is a privileged and protected member of society. Yet so often he abuses that freedom by silencing his own prophetic conscience.

Fortunately there are stories of prophetic splendor which come from the modern church. Under Hitler in Germany it was the Confessional Church which almost alone bore a faithful witness to justice and compassion. Niemöller, Bonhoeffer, Schneider, and all who stood with them reclaimed the German church from ignominy and shame.

In America today, the Christian led struggle for racial justice has become one of the noblest Christian movements in all history. Martin Luther King, Jr., and the hosts of ministers of the church, Negro and white, who flocked to Selma, Alabama, will make the mission of Jesus easier to proclaim a century from now. The choice of nonviolence as the chosen method, built as it is on Christian insights, is containing evil even as it destroys it.

The Christian church must fight on two fronts. Its first task is to link men and women individually to God as it proclaims the reconciling power of Jesus Christ. No less at the center of its message is the call to fashion a world

110

fit for the sons and daughters of God to live in. To neglect one or other of these truths is to preach half a gospel.

Christians in the main confine a prophetic ministry to official pronouncements or leave the witness to a relatively few inspired individuals. Local churches so often fail to come to grips prophetically with the issues of the community in which they are set or to fashion a Christian conscience on the larger questions of national and world life.

At the Central Methodist Mission in Sydney there is held at 3 P.M. every Sunday a gathering which is virtually a national platform on public issues. There Sunday by Sunday current affairs form the subject matter. There is a constant attempt to fashion a Christian conscience in the community, remembering that the greatness of a church is in part determined by the conscience it creates amid its people.

Titles chosen reflect the purpose of the meeting. Here are some of them: "Stop Hydrogen Bomb Tests Now," "Modify White Australia," "A New Policy on the Liquor Issue," "Personal Freedom and National Security," "Conscription or Peace," "Human Compassion and Capital Punishment," "Abandon Apartheid in South Africa," "Christian Education Demonstration."

In the main, convinced Christians are the speakers. The aim is proclamation rather than the forum or discussion approach. So often, even when the church tackles public issues, it presents its case in such a way as to cancel out any effective witness to the people. Where possible the point of view expressed picks up the prophetic pronouncements of Australian Methodism or the Australian

111

Council of Churches and gives them currency. The prophetic function of the church is thus added to the activities of the church which worships, serves, and evangelizes. Without it, the message of the church loses its balance and purpose. Through press, radio, and television the witness of this national platform is carried across Australia, and at times, beyond.

There is in the Bible what may be called the New Testament Charter of Human Rights. Centuries before the emergence of the twentieth century charter of the United Nations the Bible grappled with the basic issues of human justice and freedom.

Where is it to be found? In that great book of freedom, Galatians. The charter for the Christian prophet in society is in the third chapter: "There is neither Jew nor Greek, there is neither slave nor free, there is neither male nor female, for you are all one in Christ Jesus" (Gal. 3:28).

"There is neither Jew nor Greek." Here is the Christian challenge to racialism in all its forms. In one sentence it proclaims the consequence of the Christian understanding of God who created all men free and equal, who redeemed all men through Christ, who destines all mankind to a common immortality.

What a different story would have been written if only the church had believed its own charter. Slavery, colonialism, segregation have all emerged because neither the church nor the world has accepted the truth: "There is neither Jew nor Greek, for all are one in Christ Jesus."

"There is neither male nor female." The liberation of womanhood is far from complete. Unjust dual standards which discriminate against women remain in all societies.

112

The unmarried mother-to-be is judged more harshly than the father of her child. The deserted wife, often left with little children, needs greater protection from the man who has abandoned her. Economic injustice persists where women receive less pay than men for equal work —although the family responsibilities of a man where he is the breadwinner in the home must also be taken into account.

Through scientific birth control God is offering to womanhood new freedom and self-determination. A wife has the right to be relieved of the anxiety of having unwanted children and to share with her husband un-clouded joy in married relationships.

Birth control fulfills rather than denies the will of God. When practiced with self-discipline it can be and is thoroughly Christian. This is the liberating message the Christian prophet in society today can proclaim.

Roman Catholicism rightly fears the increasing sexuality of the world. Undoubtedly, freedom can become license but the only road is forward into acceptance of the new responsibilities which freedom demands. The whole Christian church must rejoice in the liberation from anxiety and fear which scientific methods of birth control represent for the women of the world.

"There is neither slave nor free." Political freedom has largely been won in the West. Economic freedom has not by any means dawned for masses of western people, while it remains a distant and tantalizing dream for hundreds of millions in underdeveloped countries.

If there is any area in which the prophet in society needs to be heard, it concerns the economic structure of society. Yet here there is all too often silence. Because of the extremism of communism and the fear of being labeled communist, any Christian critique of capitalism has died to a whisper. By a strange inversion of attitude, dislike of communism has caused a cloak of holiness to be thrown over capitalism which it does not deserve to wear.

There are deep, unsolved issues within capitalism, injustices which can never be accepted by the Christian conscience. Take for example the way in which capitalism aids the man with money, and works against little people who cannot accumulate resources. People with money can relatively easily make more money; people with none spend a lifetime struggling to own the small house in which they live.

Automation is certain to exaggerate the disparities of economic society. The riches of the machine flow disproportionately to the few. Unemployment hangs as a permanent threat over all who have only their labor to sell, with automation turning that threat into actuality.

In the presence of weaknesses such as these, the church has little to say. In the light of history the identification of the church with the economic status quo today could be as devastating as its acceptance without serious protest of the inequalities and injustices of the earlier industrial revolution.

An oversimplification of communism has betrayed the church into a negativism which has robbed it of facing prophetically one of the most momentous upsurges of history. The church has had no alternative but to oppose the materialism and militant atheism of communism.

Communism, however, is more than a movement of theoretic atheism. It represents a search for greater social and economic justice. It has gathered to itself the hopes and aspirations of countless millions of dispossessed people around the earth. Christianity has failed to distinguish between the evil that communism is and the good for which it strives.

Similarly, communism as a social movement has become inevitably and rightly identified with Russia. The world has every reason to fear the aggressive nationalism of Soviet Russia. Again, however, communism is more than imperial Russia on the march.

The Christian church, following in the main the leadership of Roman Catholicism, has been maneuvered into the position where it denies the hopes of millions for greater economic justice and appears to endorse and entrench the injustices of capitalism.

There was a creative word spoken by Father Florovsky, a Russian exile, at the Amsterdam Assembly of the World Council of Churches. He likened communism to Assyria of old which became an instrument in God's hands, a whip or scourge to awaken the complacency of Israel. He pleaded that the Christian church in East and West should listen intently to what God may be saying to his people through communism.

This plea was made in 1948, and it has not been followed. With the resurgence of the "rightest" movements in America and Australia, fear, complacency, and self-righteousness have triumphed. As a result, it is harder today than ever for Christian thinkers and preachers objectively to speak of communism. The prophetic interpretation of communism in God's ordering of history has been lost.

One day the madness of communism and extreme anti-communism will subside. Then another defeat of the church as the servant of all the people will become apparent. Another reason will be given why the Christian church should be rejected.

The world remains in bondage to war. Here there is no discrimination, for all men are held as slaves within the mentality and the system of militarism and war. Now, in a hydrogen bomb age, the Christian prophet must be heard.

The German philosopher Nietzche once said: "I shall not believe in the Redeemer of these Christians until they show me they are redeemed." Where is the sign of redemption in the acquiescence of so large a portion of the church in atomic warfare? If there is one fact which strains my faith in and allegience to the church more than another, it is support the church has given to Hiroshima, to hydrogen bomb testing, to stockpiling of atomic weapons, and to tacit acceptance of their use should war come.

I am ashamed, for example, that it was Earl Russell, an avowed atheist, and not a Christian leader, who should lead the passive protests in England against a nuclear holocaust—though I know some Christians take their place in the ongoing struggle against the acceptance of nuclear warfare.

Should war come, whole cities will perish—women, children, the aged—so that none shall escape, no not one. The church contemplates so complete a descent to barbarism, yet has not started back in horror. Too often it has endorsed preparations for nuclear warfare, making inevitable the solemn condoning of hydrogen bomb warfare should hostilities commence.

A prophetic church is needed urgently, desperately on the issue of peace and war in a nuclear age. If ever the conscience and compassion of Christ should find expression through the church, it is in the face of the threat of nuclear destruction. Where is that church? It is all too timid and silent. No wonder millions pass it by.

After hundreds of open-air meetings around the world where the people beyond the church are encountered, I know the importance of the image which the church gives on the issues of peace and war. I know the very future of the world mission of Jesus is bound up with the recovery of the prophetic function of the church amid the clash of nations.

Let me put it this way. Until modern man is convinced that the church has something to declare on the issues of the economic structure and war, he will not listen to what it has to say on redemption and eternal life.

Faith in the Holy Spirit

Mission is impossible without a vivid and compelling faith in the Holy Spirit. No man ever converted anybody. The renewal of the church cannot be brought about by human effort. The advance of the kingdom of Christ cannot be commanded by organizational man. It is the Spirit of God who is the agent in personal conversion, and who transforms the church and the world.

Out of the total spectrum of the Christian faith particular doctrines have a special relevance at various periods of history. In the times of Christian renewal some one doctrine seems to emerge with tremendous power. In the Reformation it was justification by faith which became the clarion call. With John Wesley, assurance and holiness won a response from the people.

The message which speaks to our condition today is the doctrine of the Holy Spirit. Millions of people who claim to possess some kind of belief in God are really

Deists. They declare with the top of their minds that God is, but live as though there were no God. God has no vital relationship with their lives or times and so they ignore him. He is the "up-there God," while they live "down here." The picture of a God who is identified with people, who is involved in history, is alien to them. It is this false image of God which has forced religion to the circumference of life, making Christian belief and practice appear irrelevant to the real business of living.

Deism is the inevitable consequence of a neglect of the doctrine of the Holy Spirit. This neglect is a major sin of the modern church. The doctrine of the Holy Spirit has for decades been the cinderella doctrine of the Christian church. Until recently, little has been written about the Holy Spirit. The rank-and-file Christian is more illiterate regarding this element of the Christian faith than most. The absence of a strongly held and clearly understood doctrine of the Spirit has robbed the church of clues to enable it to understand what is happening around it and made it impotent in important areas of its ministry. From it has come a static rather than a dynamic conception of God which has turned the eyes of the church inward and backward, explaining why so many of the creative movements of our time have almost passed the church by.

The neglect of the Holy Spirit in the world's major churches explains another phenomenon in the world Christian scene, the growth of the Pentecostal churches. God does not allow a vacuum to persist; he brings forth someone, some movement to fill it. Often this leads to further distortion, as protest movements often exaggerate and distort the very truths to which they bear witness.

119

So it is with pentecostalism, but that God is speaking to his church through it seems to me undeniable. God is calling us to rediscover the person and power of the Holy Spirit.

The Holy Spirit is the agent in conversion. From prevenient grace to sanctification he is the power at work in human lives. It is the Holy Spirit who produces that fundamental transformation of life which can be described by the word conversion.

The beginning and end of modern man's troubles is his estrangement from God. The supreme need of modern man is to find an end to that estrangement and to accept reconciliation with God. It is the Holy Spirit who performs this miracle and who brings about the transforming, conversion experience.

The absence of a strong faith in the Holy Spirit explains another serious loss with the modern church, the loss of faith in conversion. The modern church is satisfied if it influences people rather than changes them. Conversion, the radical transformation which Christ can bring, is not expected, hence it rarely happens.

The loss of faith in conversion is especially serious in a day when men and women are from three to four generations separated from a vital Christian knowledge and experience, as many now are in western society. As in John Wesley's day, people must be won all over again, and from far beyond any Christian knowledge or allegiance. Commitment to Christ, and the revolution in living this brings are their need.

William Russell Maltby, in *Obiter Scripta*, puts his finger at the point of weakness in a chapter entitled "The

Christian by Degrees." He tells of the earlier dramatic conversion which characterized Methodism. Now, in a reaction perhaps against looking for conversions only of the sudden and dramatic kind, he says, "The standard pattern now is the gradual Christian."

To plunge backward, especially in the history of Methodism, is to be in a very different atmosphere. Why, the early Methodist preachers were called "The Now Men." It came from the happenings on the American frontier as it moved west. In the pioneer huts, the saloons, the crude halls, and churches, the Methodist circuit riders had one message: "Behold, now is the acceptable time; behold, now is the day of salvation" (II Cor. 6:2). They called for instant commitment and offered instant conversion. And it happened. The church grew through the conversion, through the radical transformation of attitude and conduct which followed in the wake of the itinerant evangelist preacher.

I have come to believe profoundly in the value of seeking open commitment to God in Christ. For half of my ministry, while I think I preached for a verdict, I rarely sought any indication as to whether a verdict was recorded. Experience over the last decade has forced me constantly to call people to the focus of a declared decision to obey Jesus Christ. Through this new emphasis I believe far greater fruitfulness has appeared.

Every Sunday night at the Central Methodist Mission in Sydney at our theatre service, we invite people to come forward, thus openly registering acceptance of Jesus Christ. The method used is simple. At the close of the address all are asked to share in a time of silence. In it,

121

people are asked to make their silent dedication by repeating the sentence: "I commit my life to Jesus Christ in the fellowship of his Church."

As the final hymn is sung, all who have made a commitment to Christ for the first time in their lives are invited to come forward to accept a commitment card. Several ushers and counselors move forward at the same time to break the aloneness of those who come and to accompany them to a counseling room. Through obtaining an open confession of faith, follow-up procedures, which allow for pastoral care and Christian nurture, operate.

I admit, of course, that a downtown service, in a theater, always has present scores or hundreds of people who are not known to us. This explains why rarely a Sunday night passes without some making the great choice. From the results obtained I know that the procedures we follow are for our situation right. By the Sunday open offering of Christ at worship, which is the climax of all the witness and service of the week, the church grows.

In settled neighborhood churches, a weekly call for commitment and conversion would be unwise. However, it is equally wrong to go, year after year, without at least at intervals giving people the opportunity for open commitment.

Many are the conversion stories which could be told, especially if confidences could be broken. One must be sufficient. In response to an appeal there came one night a Fijian seaman. His ship was in port for the weekend. Somehow, walking the lonely streets, he turned into the lighted theatre. There by open commitment he accepted Jesus Christ as Savior and Lord.

Two years later, when in Fiji, I learned the consequence of that decision. A growing thirst for liquor was arrested, and a breaking marriage was restored. Now a lay preacher and leader in his local church, his influence is real and deep. It all began on the night in Sydney when he not merely entered a church, but was there—and I do not hesitate to use the word—converted.

If I could say only one thing to modern preachers it would be, Preach for a verdict. In an age when millions live perpetually beyond any Christian experience, pray, expect, and work for conversions. Above all, believe in the Holy Spirit, the agent in conversion.

The Holy Spirit is at work in the world. Away beyond organized religion, outside church buildings, wherever people are to be found, there the Spirit of God works.

In the secular structures of society, the influence, the Spirit of God is seen. The report of the 1963 Mexico meeting of the Commission on World Mission and Evangelism of the World Council of Churches points vividly to this truth.

"Drunkards are reformed in Alcoholics Anonymous, lives broken by fear and anxiety find healing in a group therapy session in a hospital, homes torn apart by jealousies and conflicts find new unity at a Marriage Counselling Agency, families almost dehumanized by overcrowded tenements are restored to better human relationships by a city council's imaginative rehousing scheme, young lives stultified by disabilities imposed upon a particular class or race are lifted into dignity by social and political reform."

The Spirit of God is at work in the vast movements

which today move like the surge of a tidal wave through mankind. Some see in these movements a vast plot of communism or an expression of something else which is presumed to be evil. I rather see in them the workings of God. It is God who cries for deliverance in the voice of the "freedom marcher." It is God who struggles among the dispossessed of the earth as they seek a higher quality of economic justice than capitalism has been able to give. It is God who can be heard shouting his protest who can endure no longer the obscenity and blasphemy of war.

Humanity is on the march. We are living through one of the noblest advance periods of history. God is creating a new world under our eyes and it is marvelous in our sight.

I celebrate the greatness of a God who has called mankind to unceasing warfare against pauperism, hunger, and illiteracy.

I celebrate the greatness of God who leads the non-white peoples of the earth to freedom in a movement akin to that which brought slavery to an end.

I celebrate the greatness of a God who is setting us on the road to deliverance from the worst scourge of all history, war.

I celebrate the greatness of a God who is beginning to bring to new, almost miraculous unity, Protestants and Roman Catholics and who is fashioning a new Christendom composed not of territories but of people of all lands whose heart is fixed on Christ.

Let it be said, boldly and bluntly that the "winds of change" are the breath of God.

The Holy Spirit equips and empowers all who believe

124

in him. He is the strength of the preacher, the guide of all who labor in the servant church, the wisdom of the layman witnessing in the world, the courage of the prophet.

There is an experience of the Holy Spirit which has eluded so many of us. The sentence above all else we need to hear appears in the challenge Paul gave to disciples of Jesus he found at Ephesus: "Did you receive the Holy Spirit when you believed?" The answer many a Christian would almost have to give is the same as then: "No, we have never even heard that there is a Holy Spirit" (Acts 19:2).

There came a moment in my life which transformed my whole ministry. It happened this way.

In 1953 I was chosen by the General Conference of the Methodist Church in Australia to lead "The Mission to the Nation." Launching date for the crusade, which was to be the largest effort ever undertaken by the Australian church, was April 6. As the day drew near I shrank back, overwhelmed by a sense of impotence and inadequacy.

To prepare for the mission I went to a small house, set between the sea and the Australian bush. On the night before the launching meeting in Melbourne, I walked amid the tall, white, gum trees which stretched behind our home.

Presently, on the warm, dry grass between two towering trees which stood like sentinels in the moonlight, I lay down and tried to pray. Suddenly I became aware that a wind had sprung up. I could hear it, rustling in the leaves of the gum trees above me.

125

From nowhere came the memory of another evening long ago in Palestine. It was the night when Nicodemus came to Jesus. I could imagine the scene. Jesus was speaking to Nicodemus of the mystery of the Spirit. "Unless one is born of water and the Spirit, he cannot enter the kingdom of God," said Jesus (John 3:5).

Nicodemus could not grasp it. Jesus walked across the room. The wind could be heard moving through the trees outside the window. "You must be born anew," Jesus said. "The wind blows where it wills, and you hear the sound of it, but you do not know whence it comes or whether it goes; so it is with every one who is born of the Spirit" (John 3:7-8).

Suddenly something happened. I was not in Palestine, but Australia. I saw the link between then and now. I too was listening to the wind, symbol of the breath of God.

"The wind is in the gum trees! The wind is in the gum trees!" The phrase pressed into my mind with compelling power. The Holy Spirit came upon me with a power I had never known before. I only know it changed my life.

At that moment, I knew that God would own and bless the Mission to the Nation. My fear departed. Next day I caught the plane to Melbourne and the mission was on. Over the next three years the promise was fulfilled. In Australia was heard the wind in the gum trees, the wind of the Spirit.

There is an experience of the Holy Spirit which awaits us all. Without it we cannot fully play our part in the world mission of Jesus. With it the church will become irresistible.

For the fulfillment of the great promise we wait. "You shall receive power when the Holy Spirit has come upon you; and you shall be my witnesses in Jerusalem and in all Judea and Samaria and to the end of the earth" (Acts 1:8).